I0489289

Aayush Creations

ADULT COLORING BOOK

Relax,
Refresh
& Rejoice
Handmade
designs

Vaishali Mane & Aayush Kumar

Copyright © 2016 Vaishali Mane & Aayush Kumar.

All rights reserved. No part of this book may be reproduced, stored, or transmitted by any
means—whether auditory, graphic, mechanical, or electronic—without written permission of
both publisher and author, except in the case of brief excerpts used in critical articles and reviews.
Unauthorized reproduction of any part of this work is illegal and is punishable by law.

ISBN: 978-1-4834-6156-4 (sc)
ISBN: 978-1-4834-6155-7 (e)

Because of the dynamic nature of the Internet, any web addresses or links contained in this book may have changed
since publication and may no longer be valid. The views expressed in this work are solely those of the author and do
not necessarily reflect the views of the publisher, and the publisher hereby disclaims any responsibility for them.

Any people depicted in stock imagery provided by Thinkstock are models,
and such images are being used for illustrative purposes only.
Certain stock imagery © Thinkstock.

Lulu Publishing Services rev. date: 12/13/2016

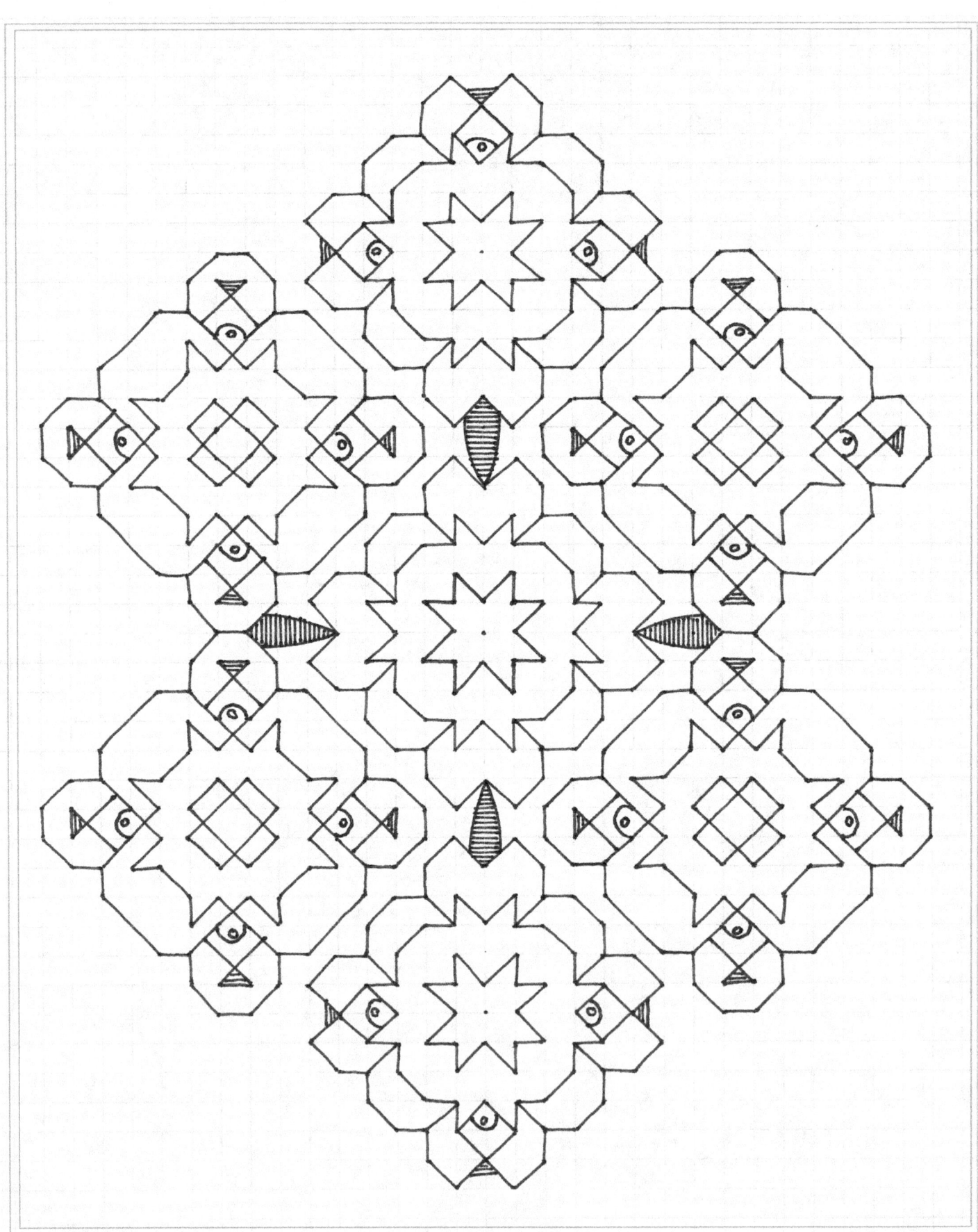

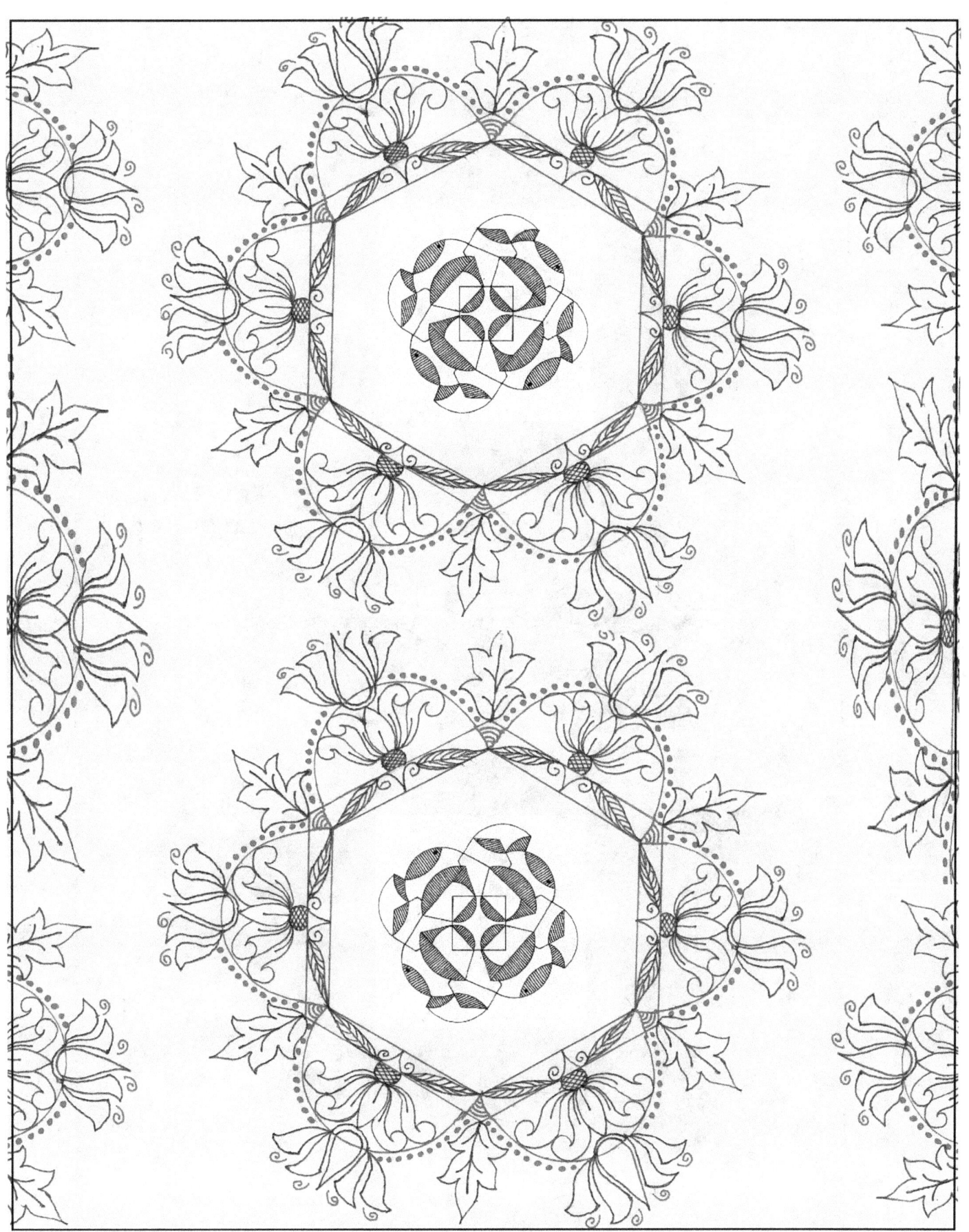

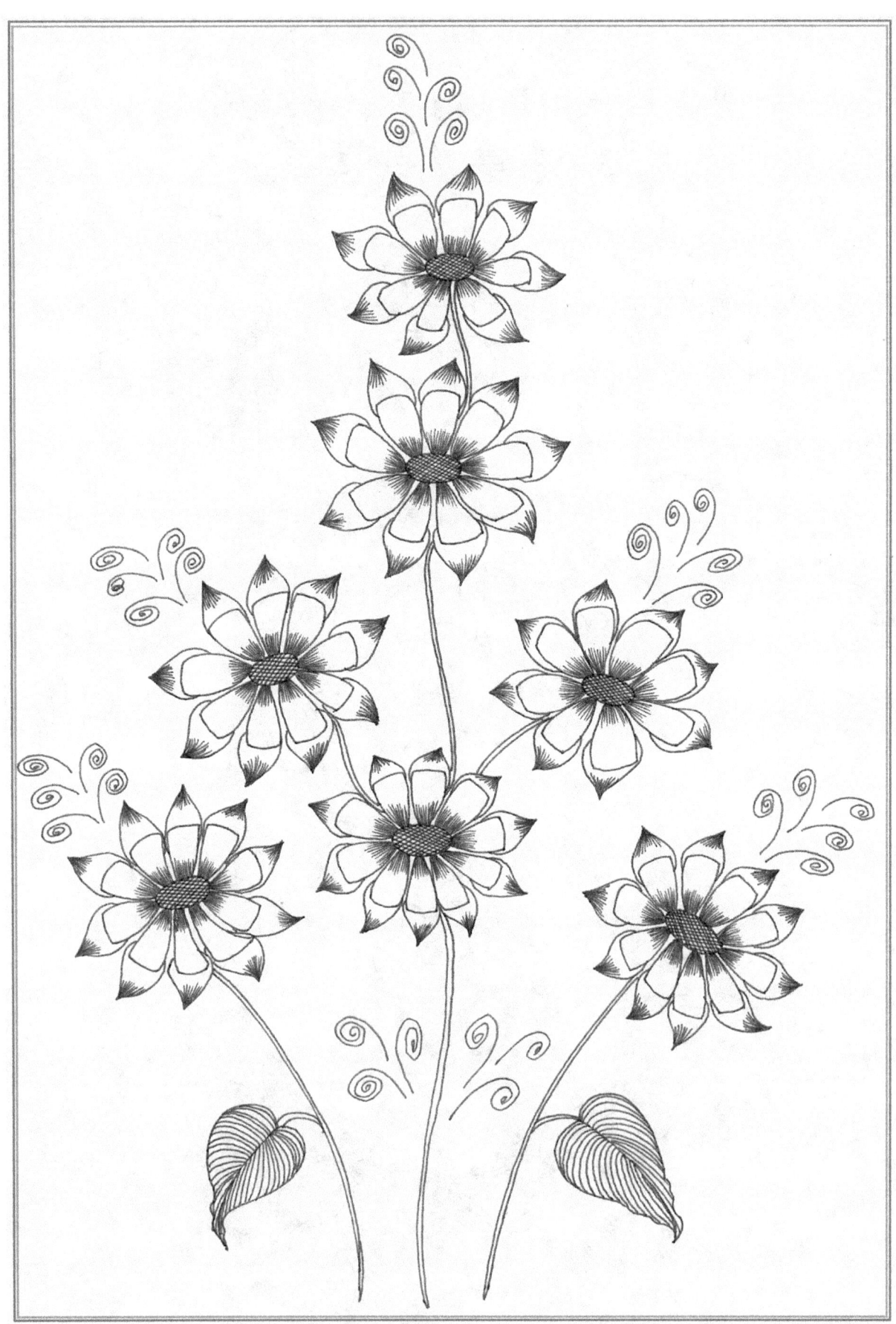

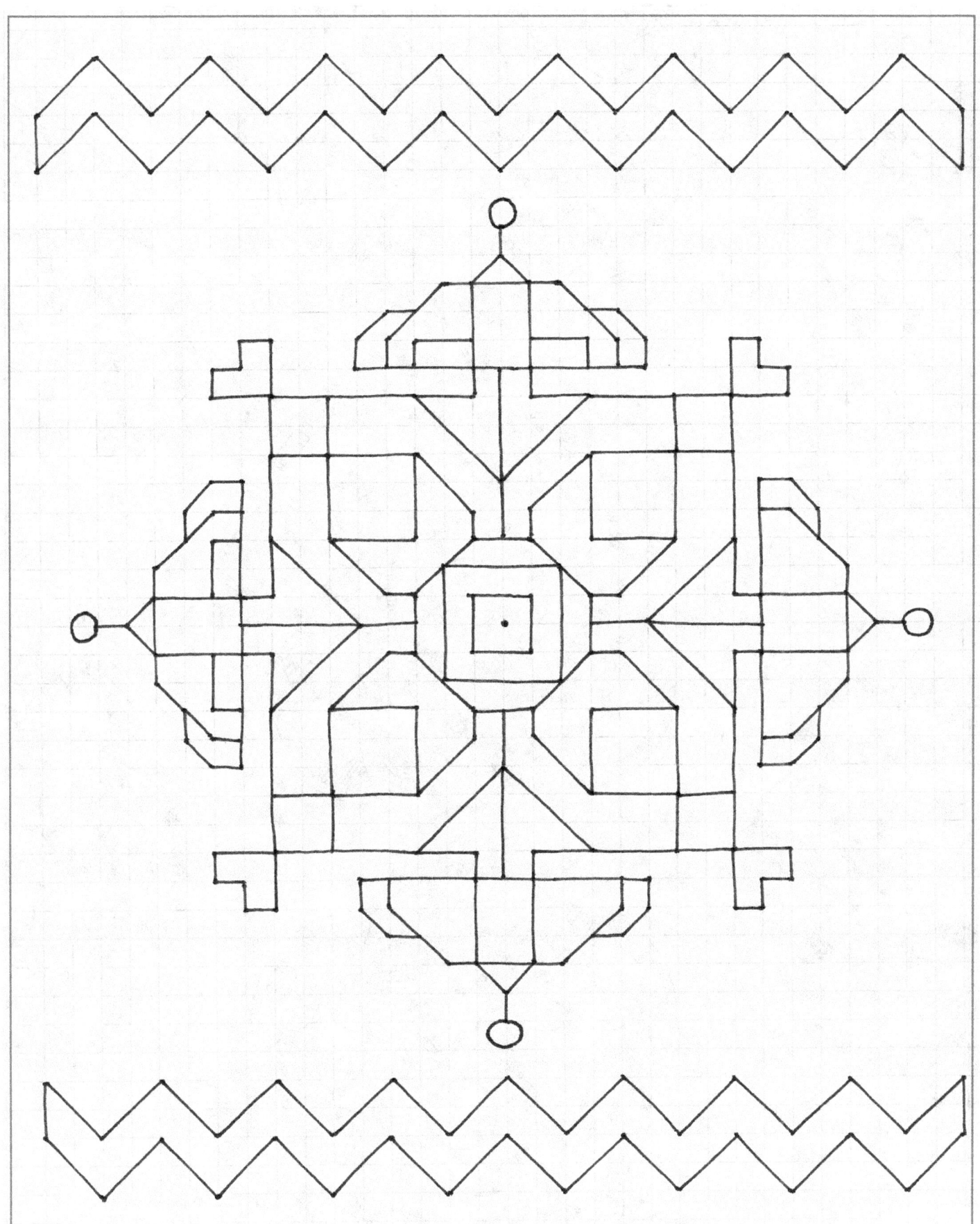

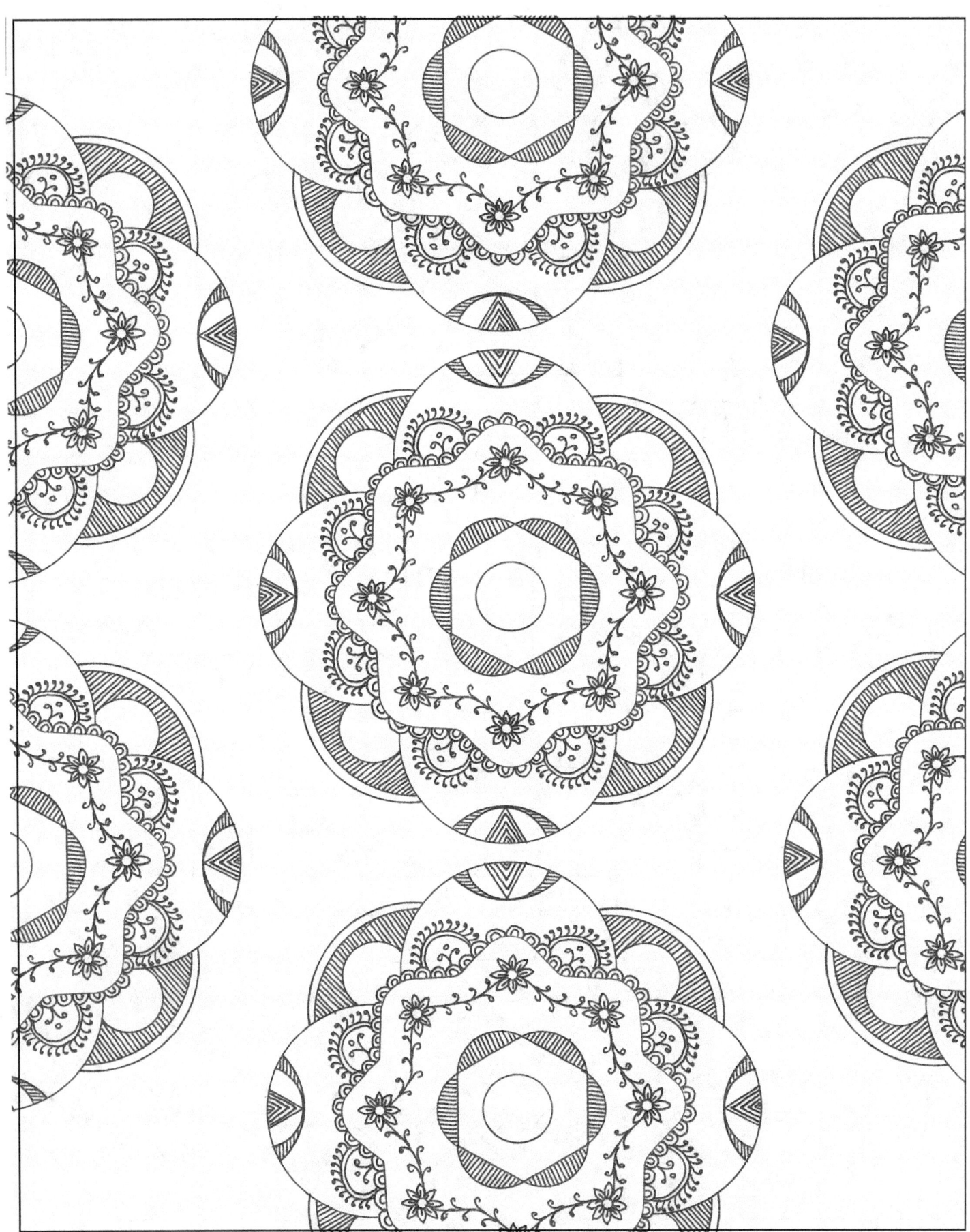

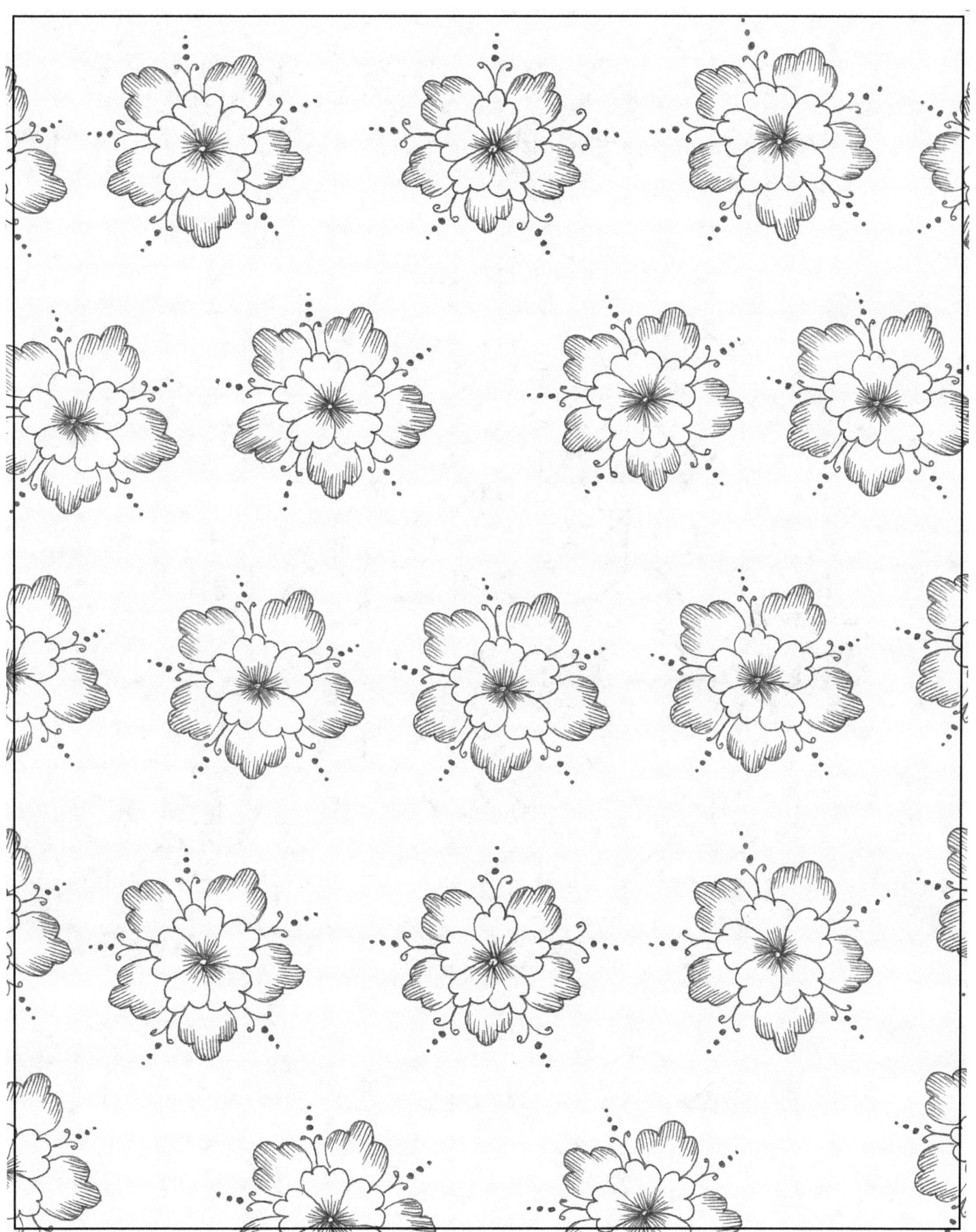

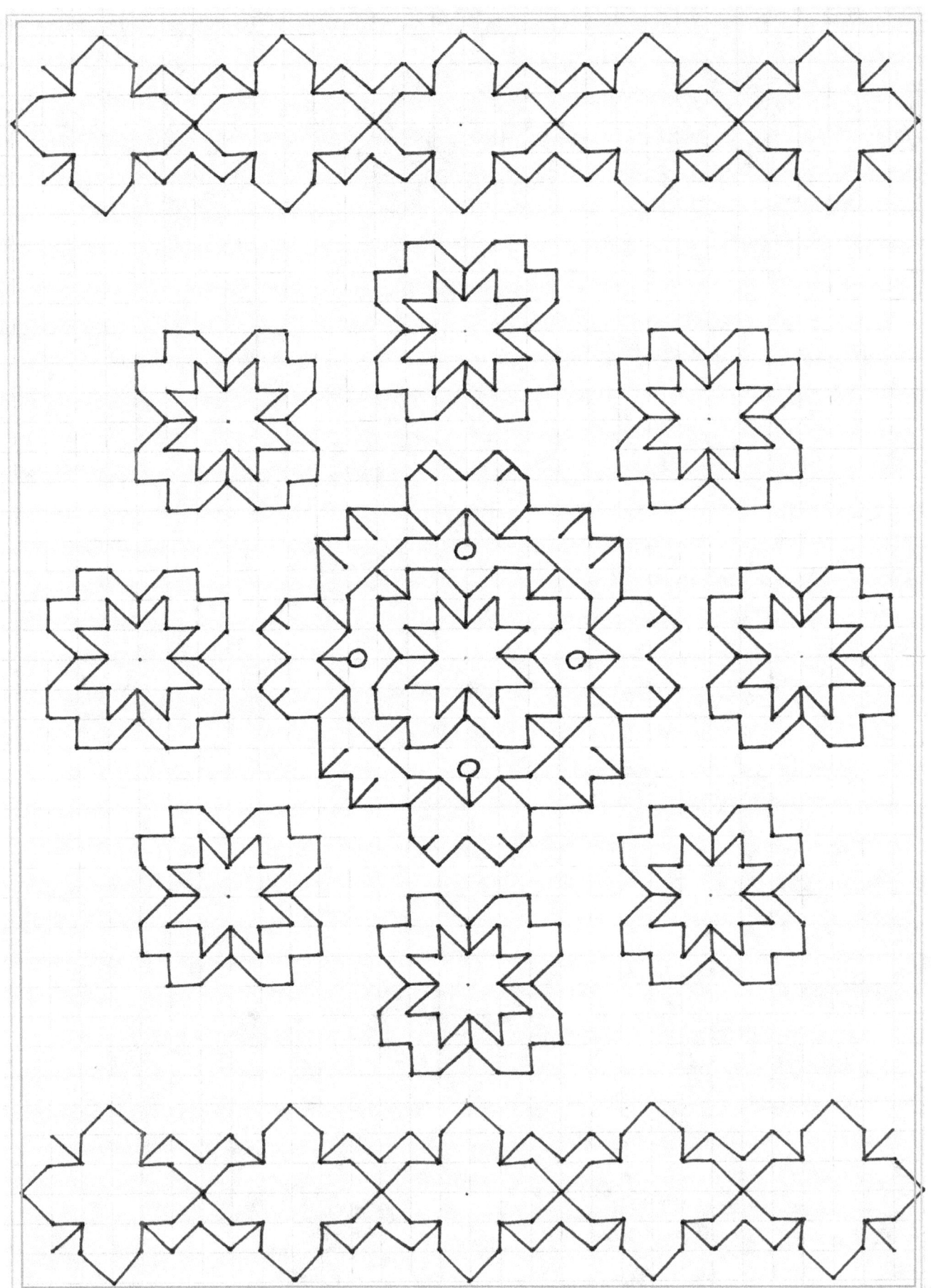

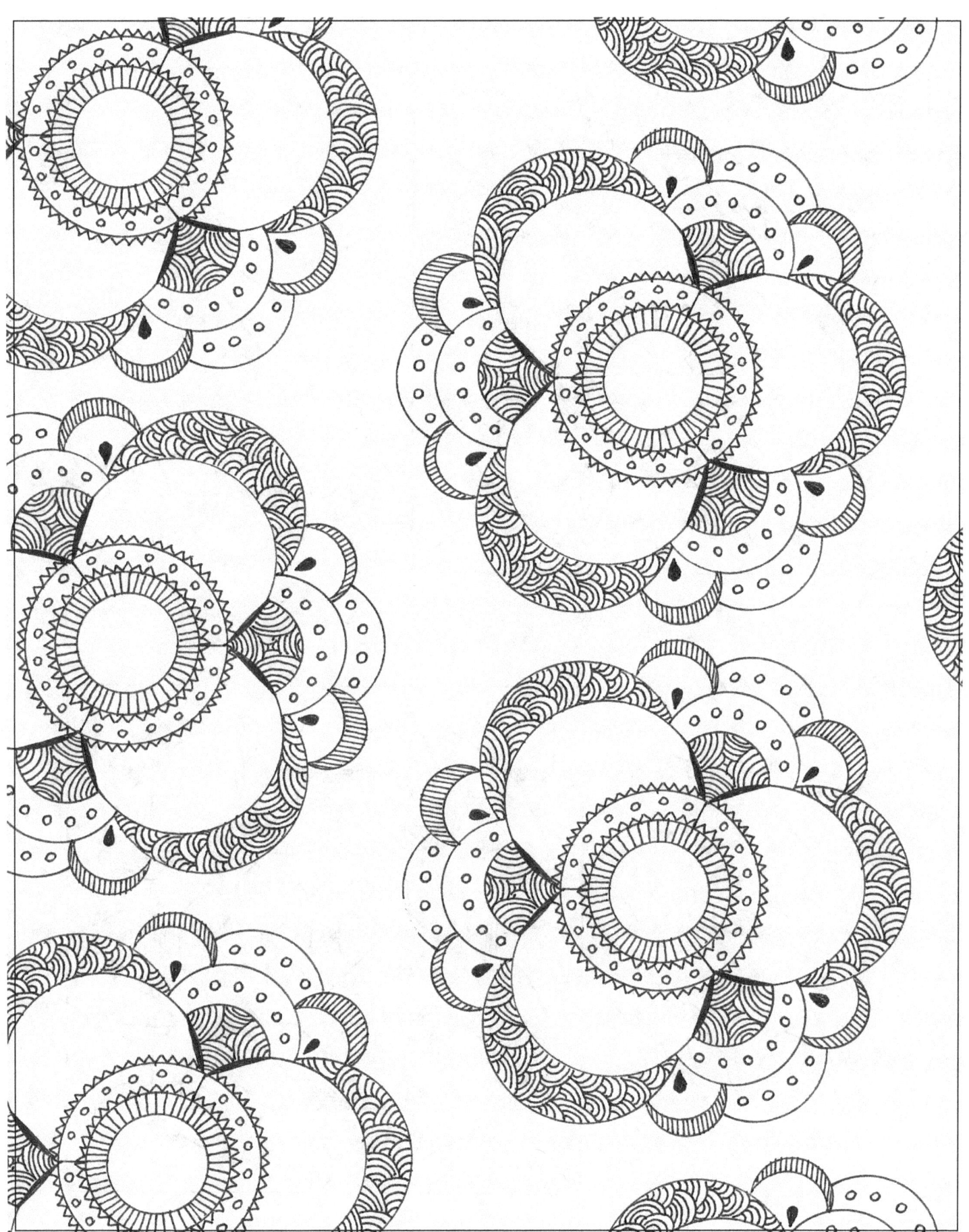

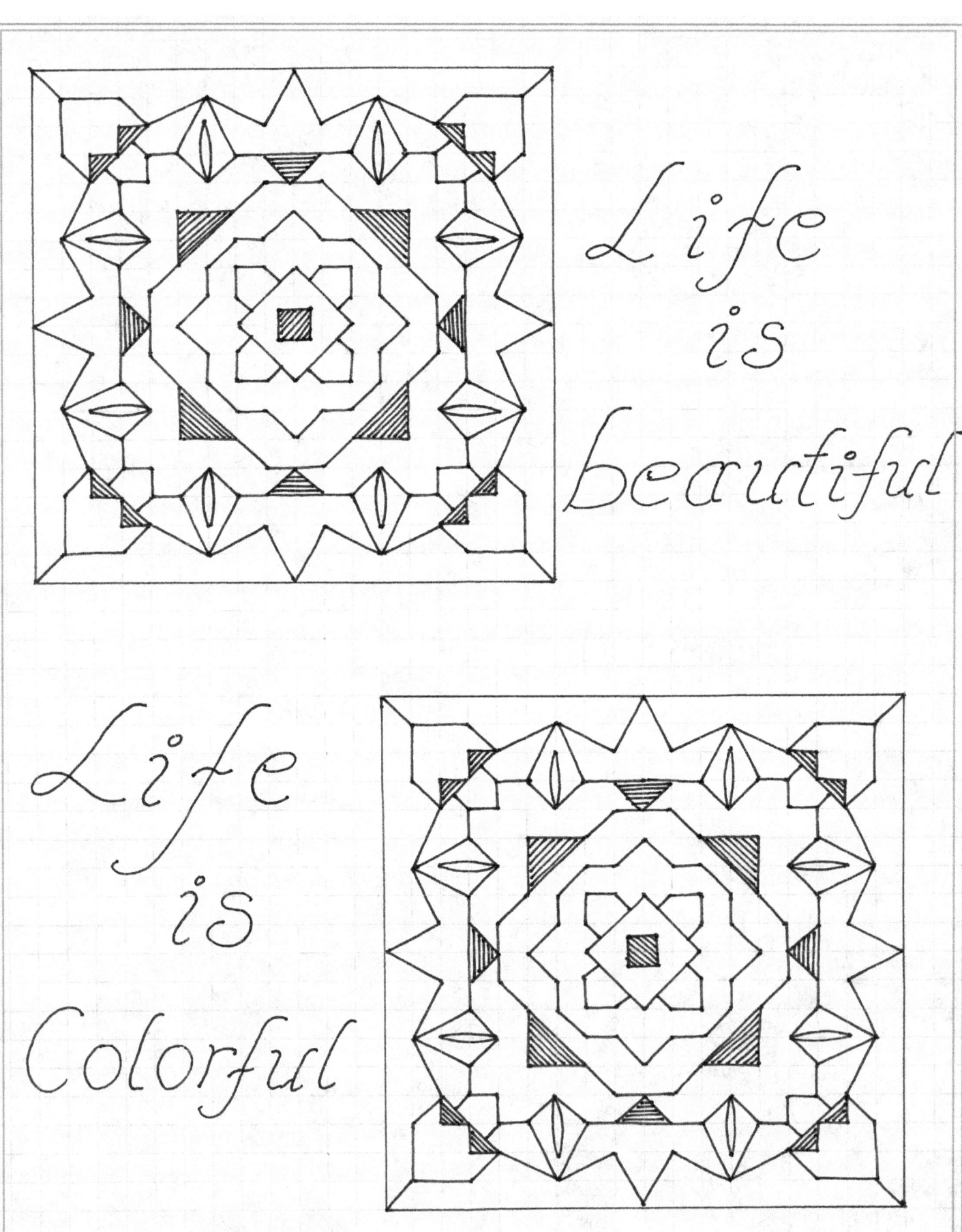

Life
is
beautiful

Life
is
Colorful

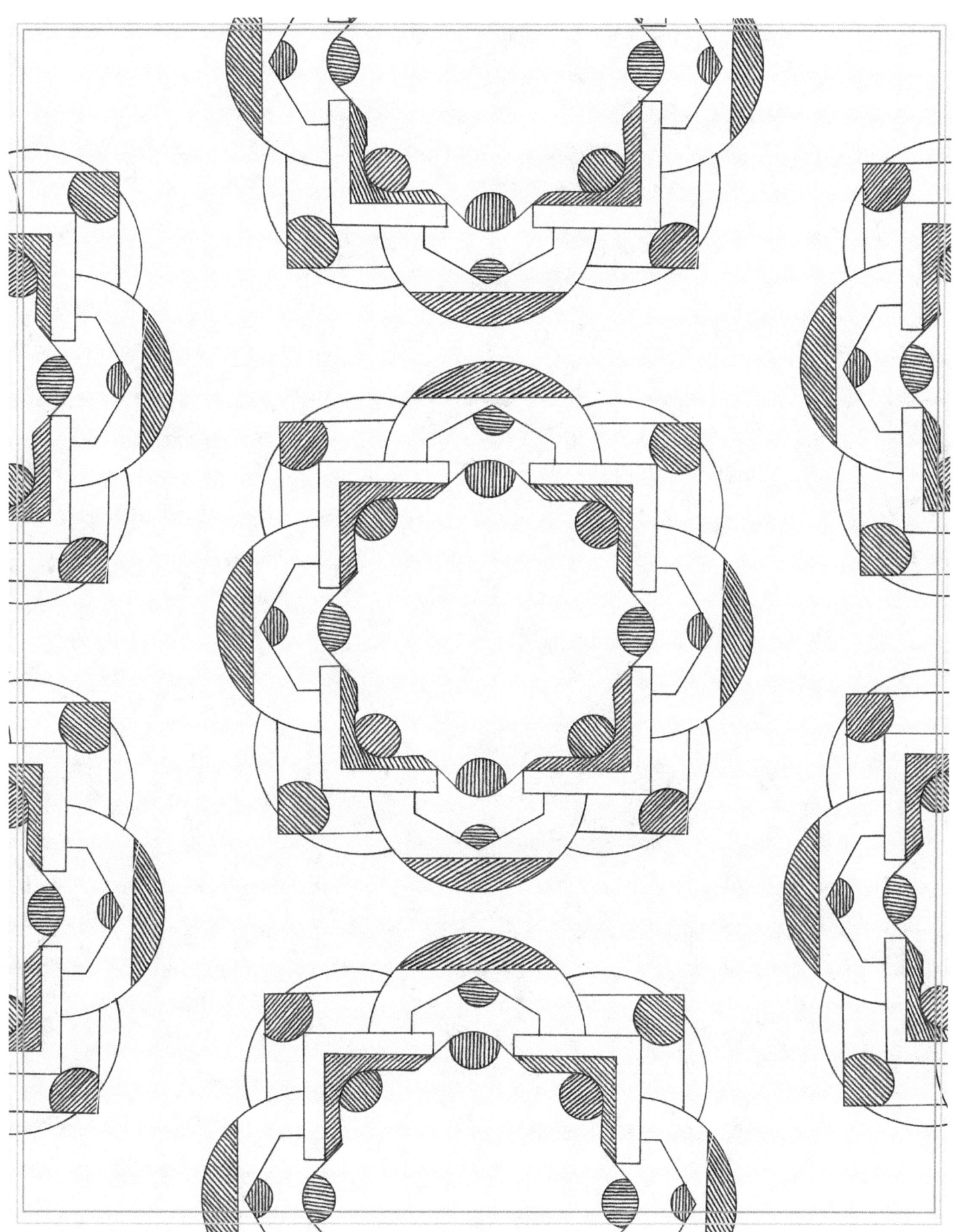

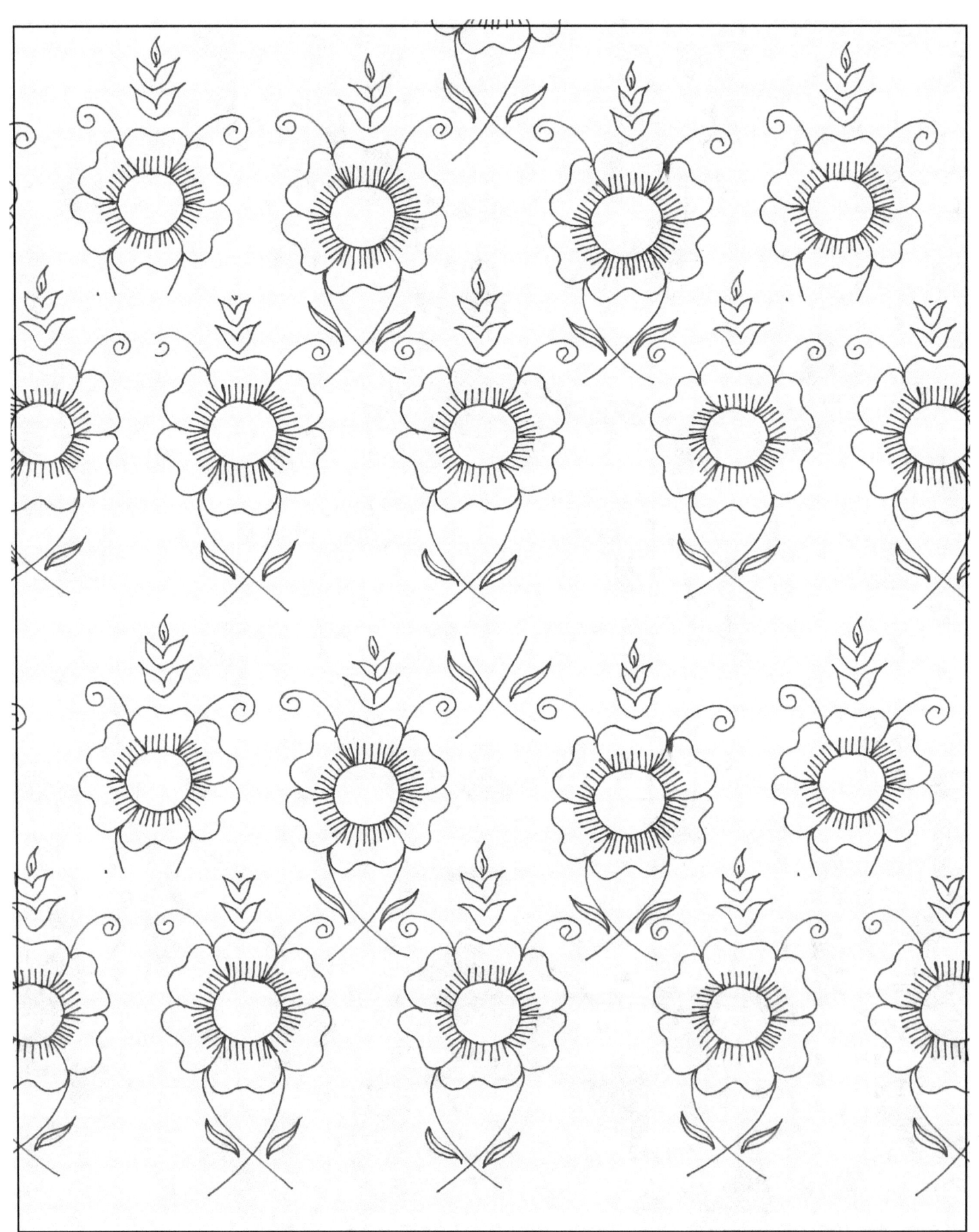

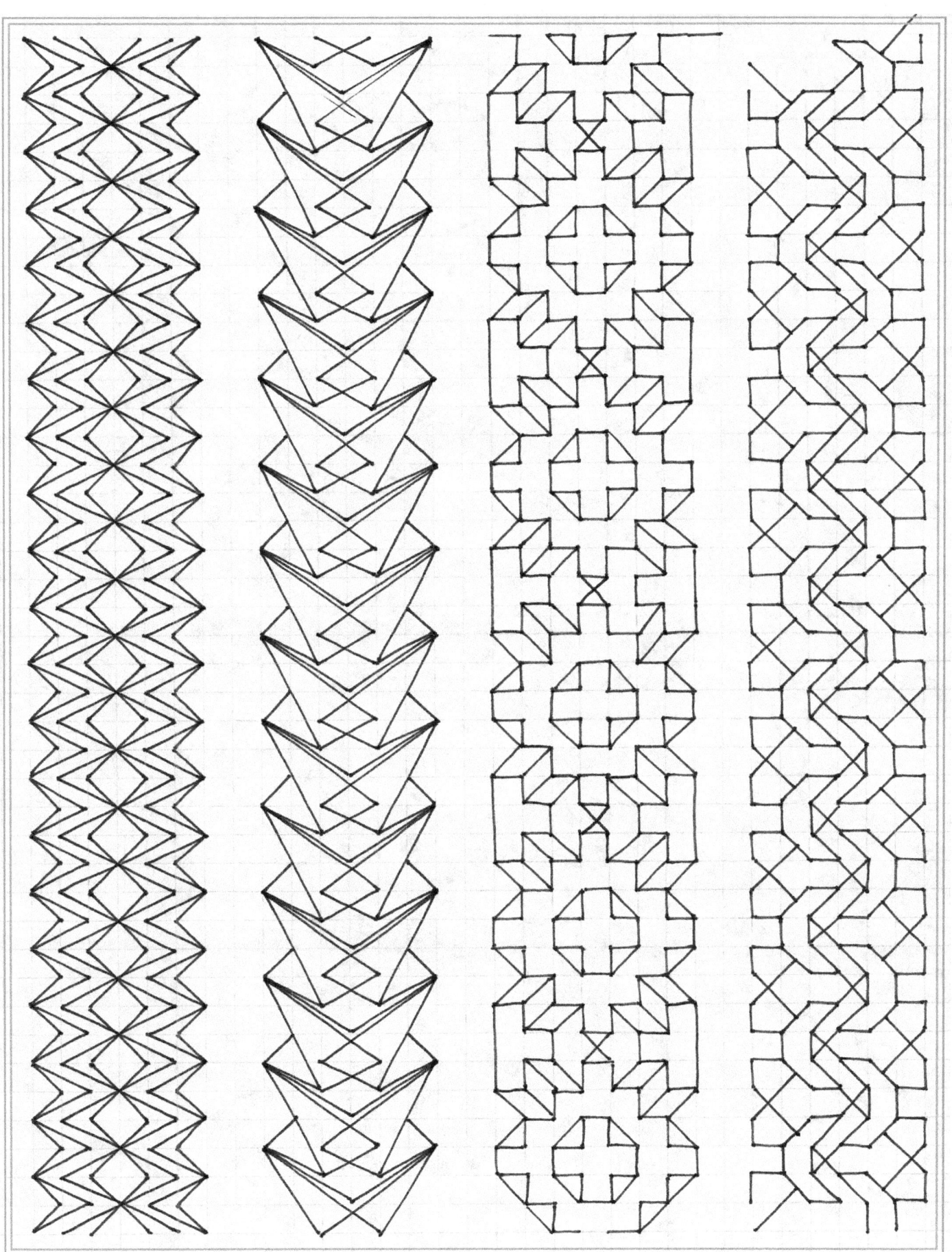

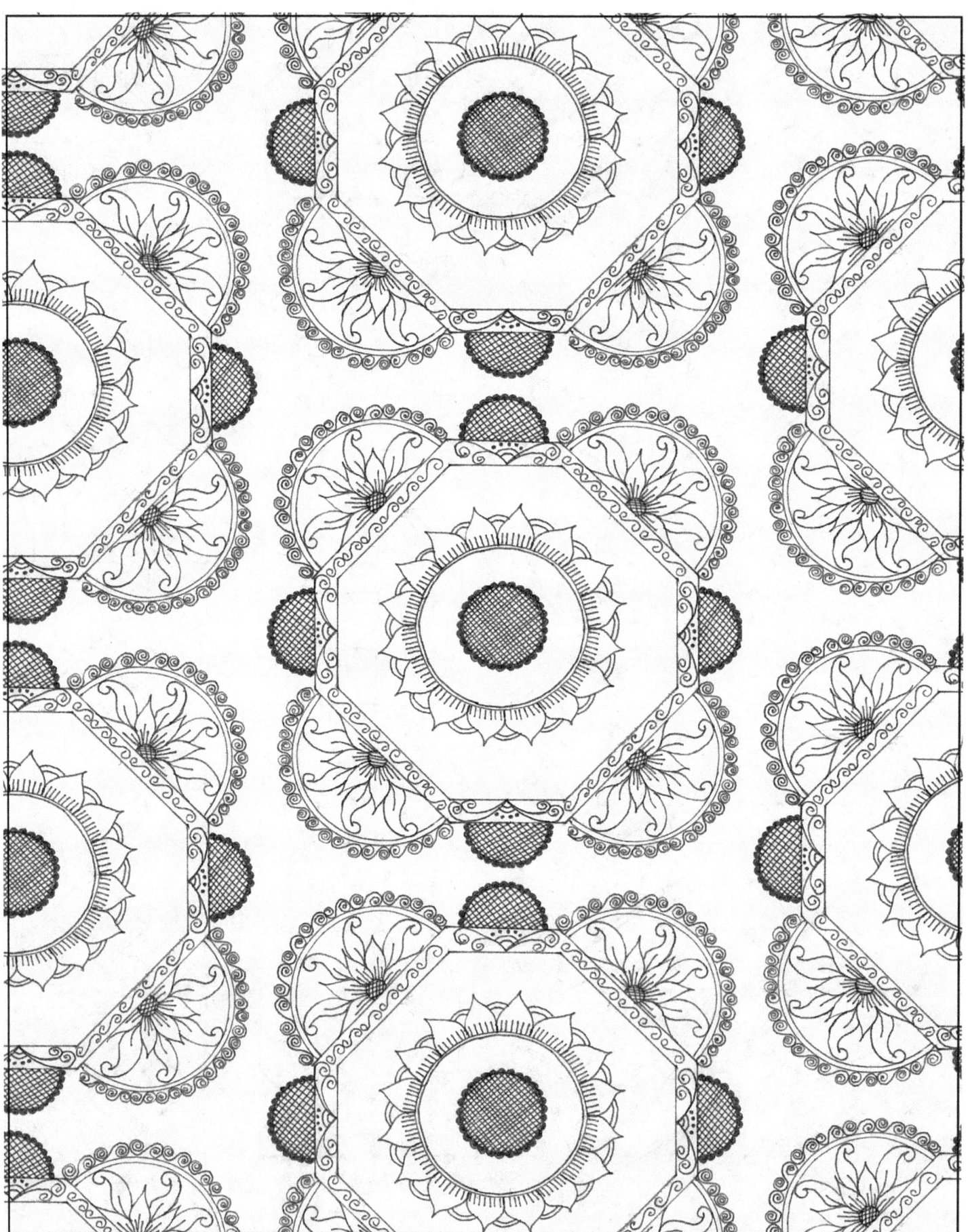

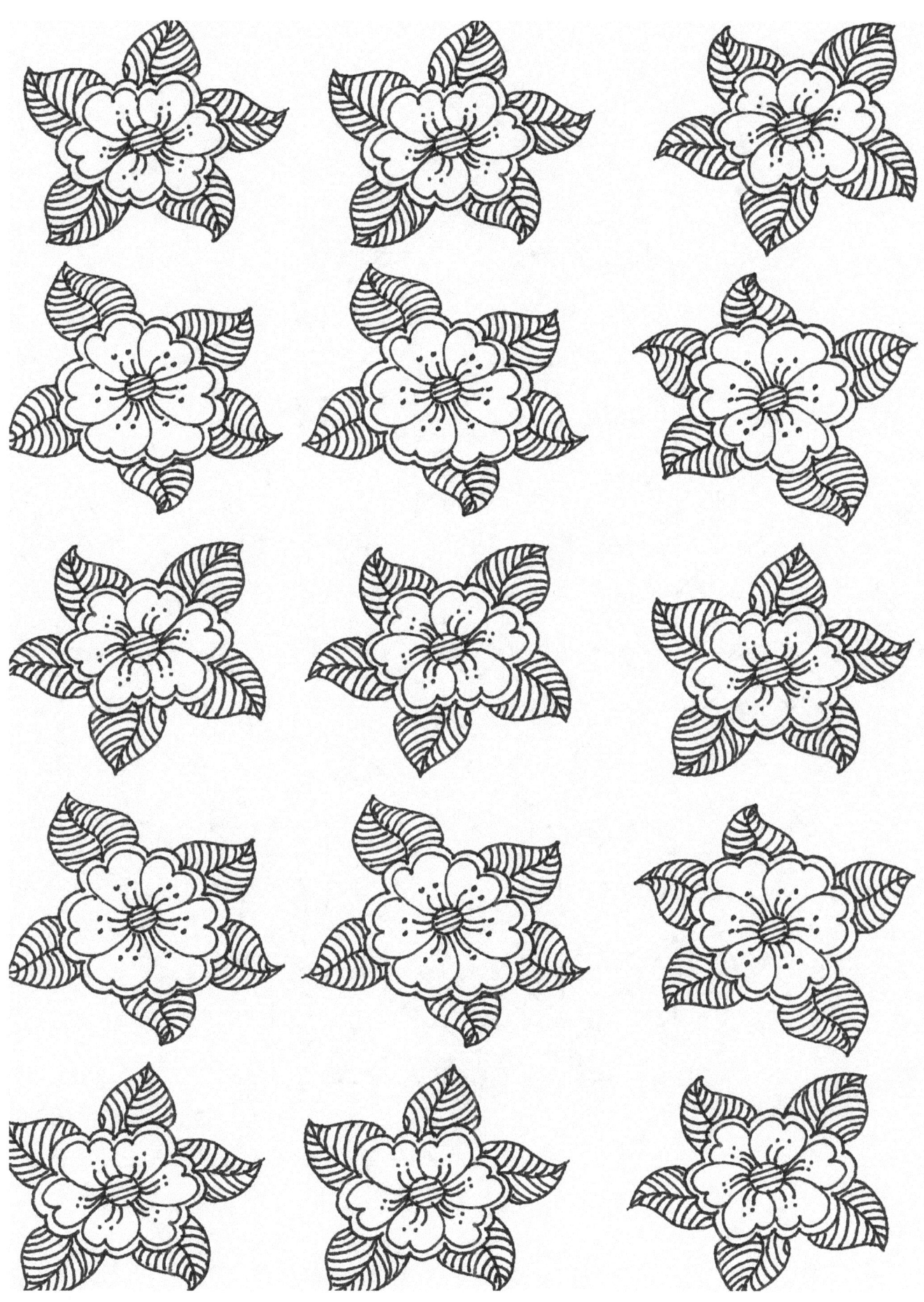

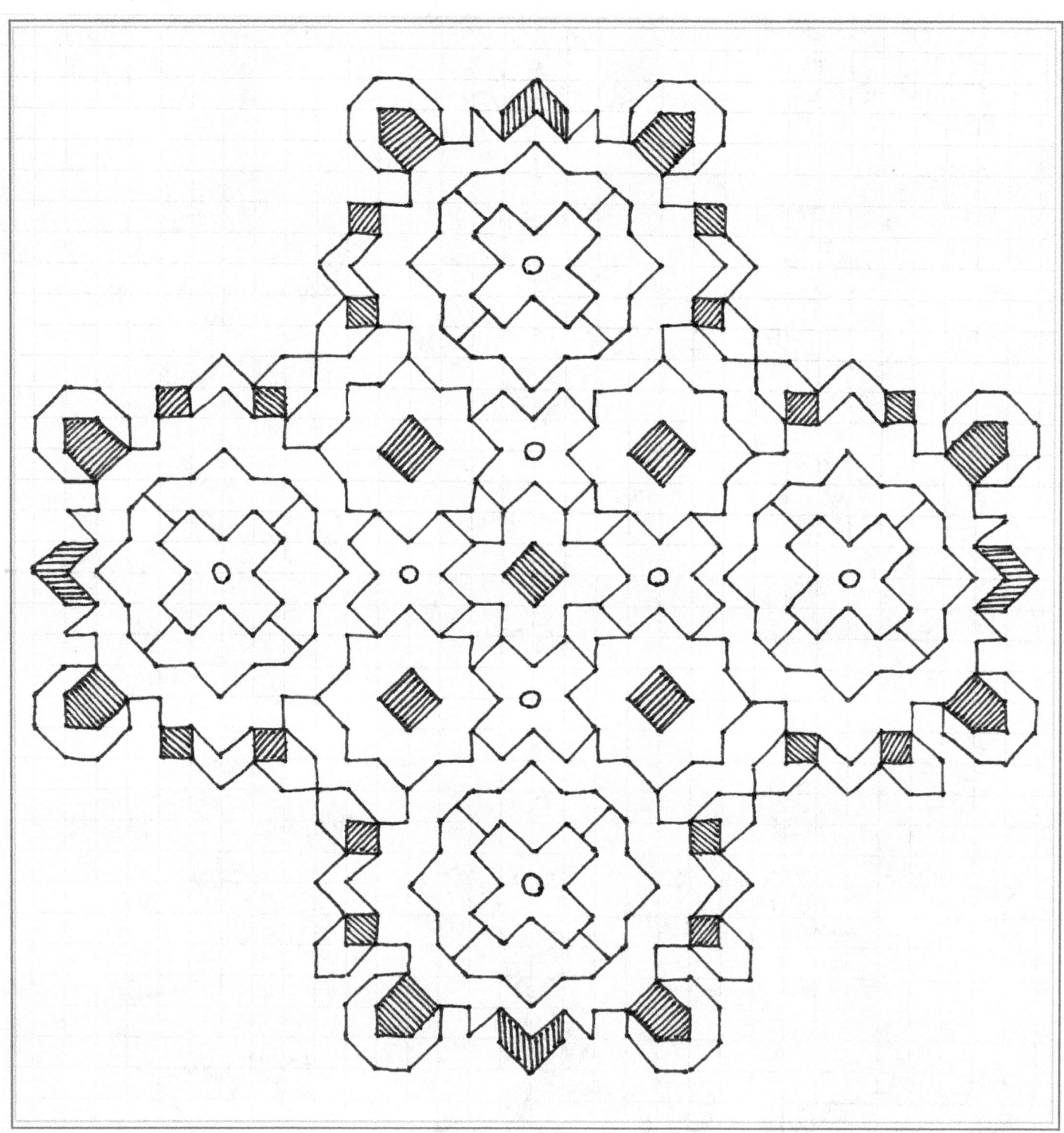

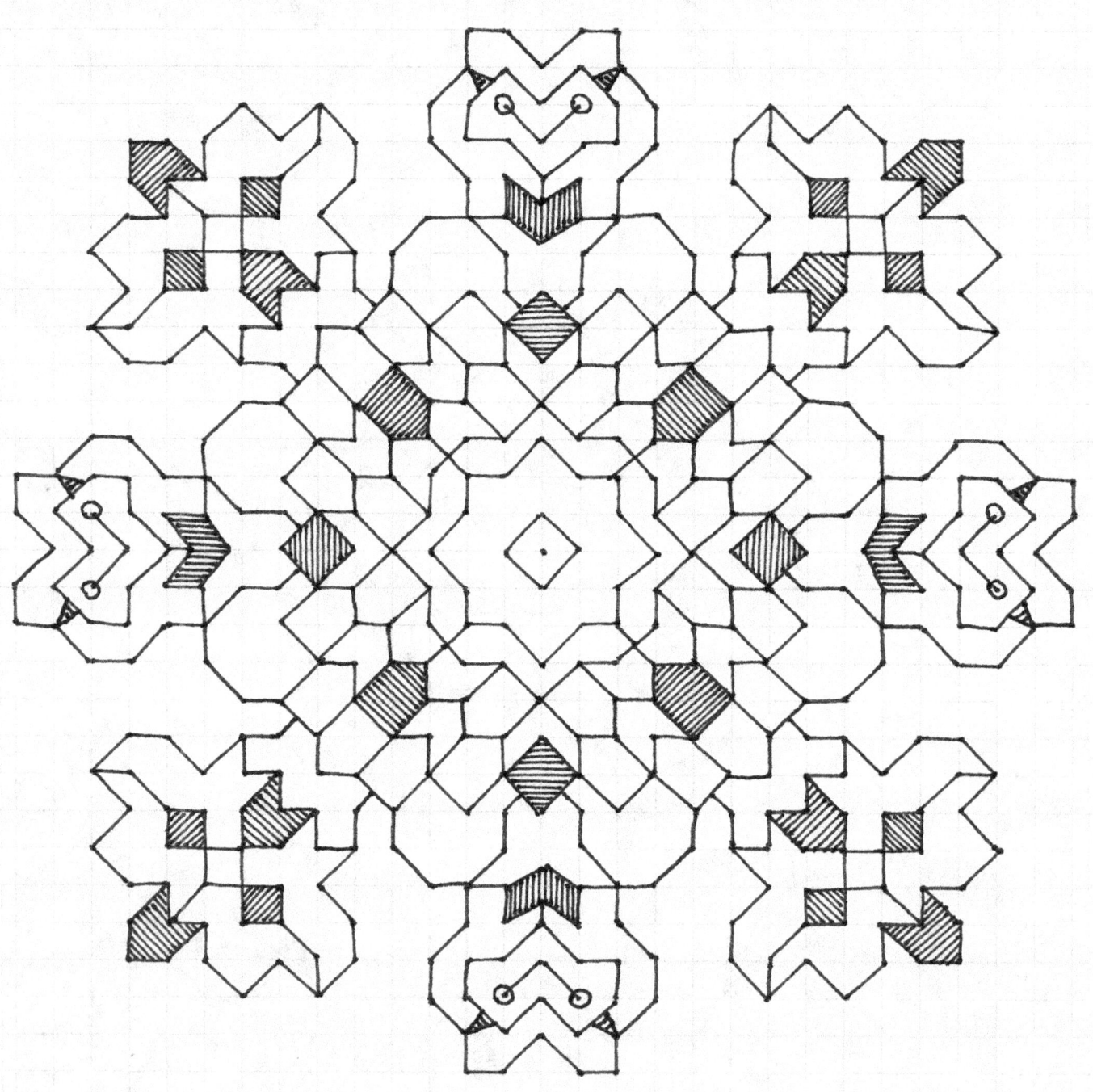

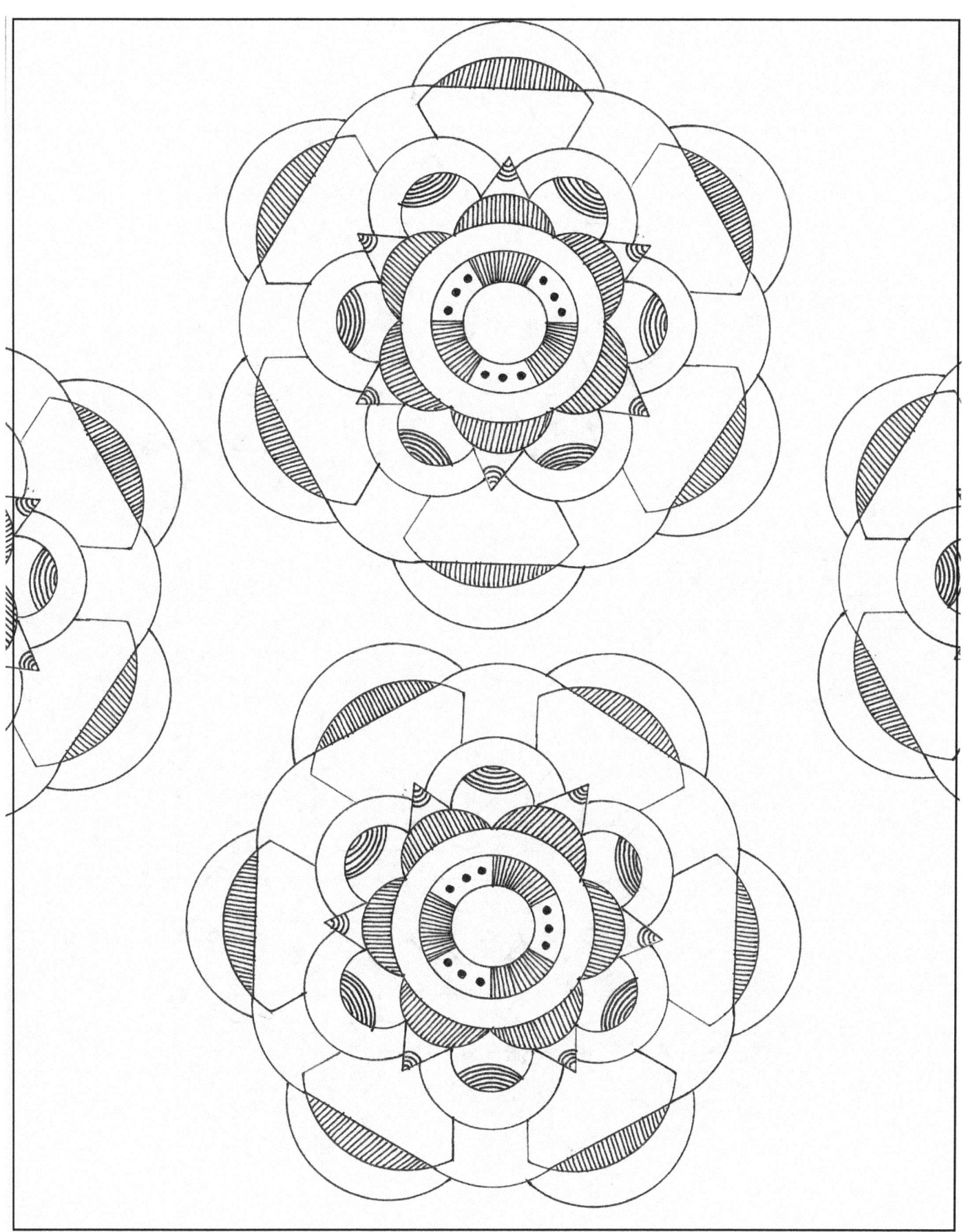

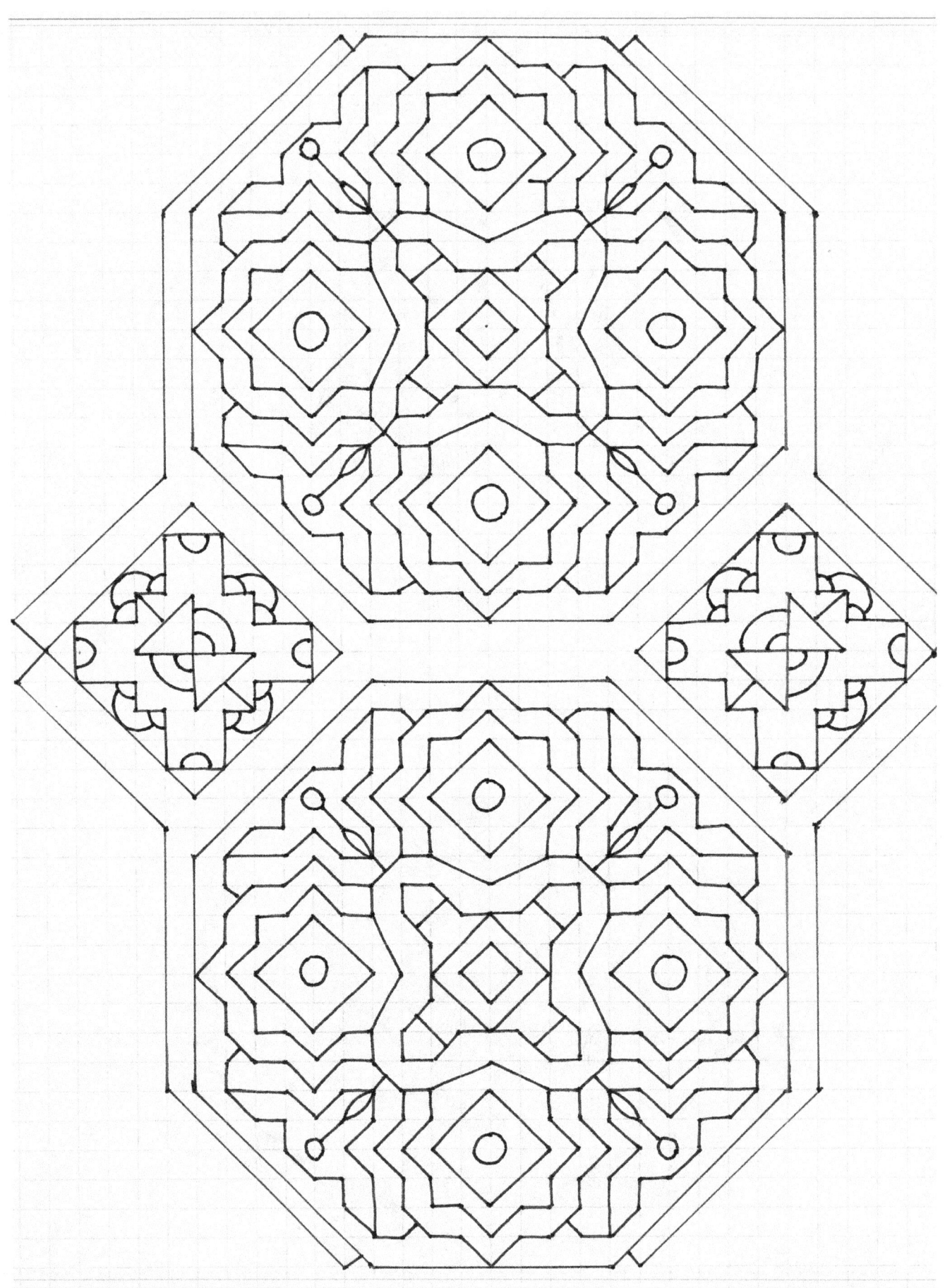

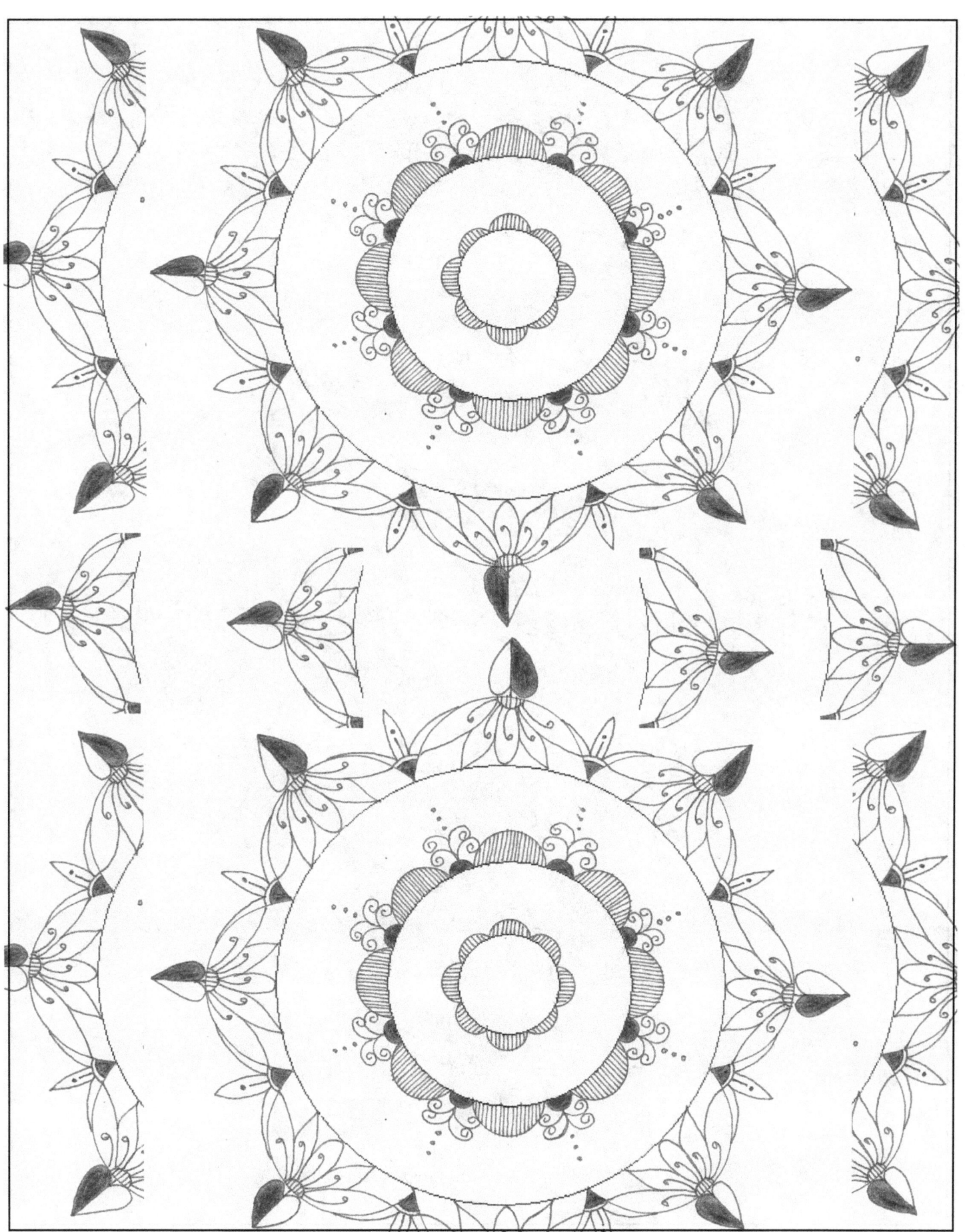

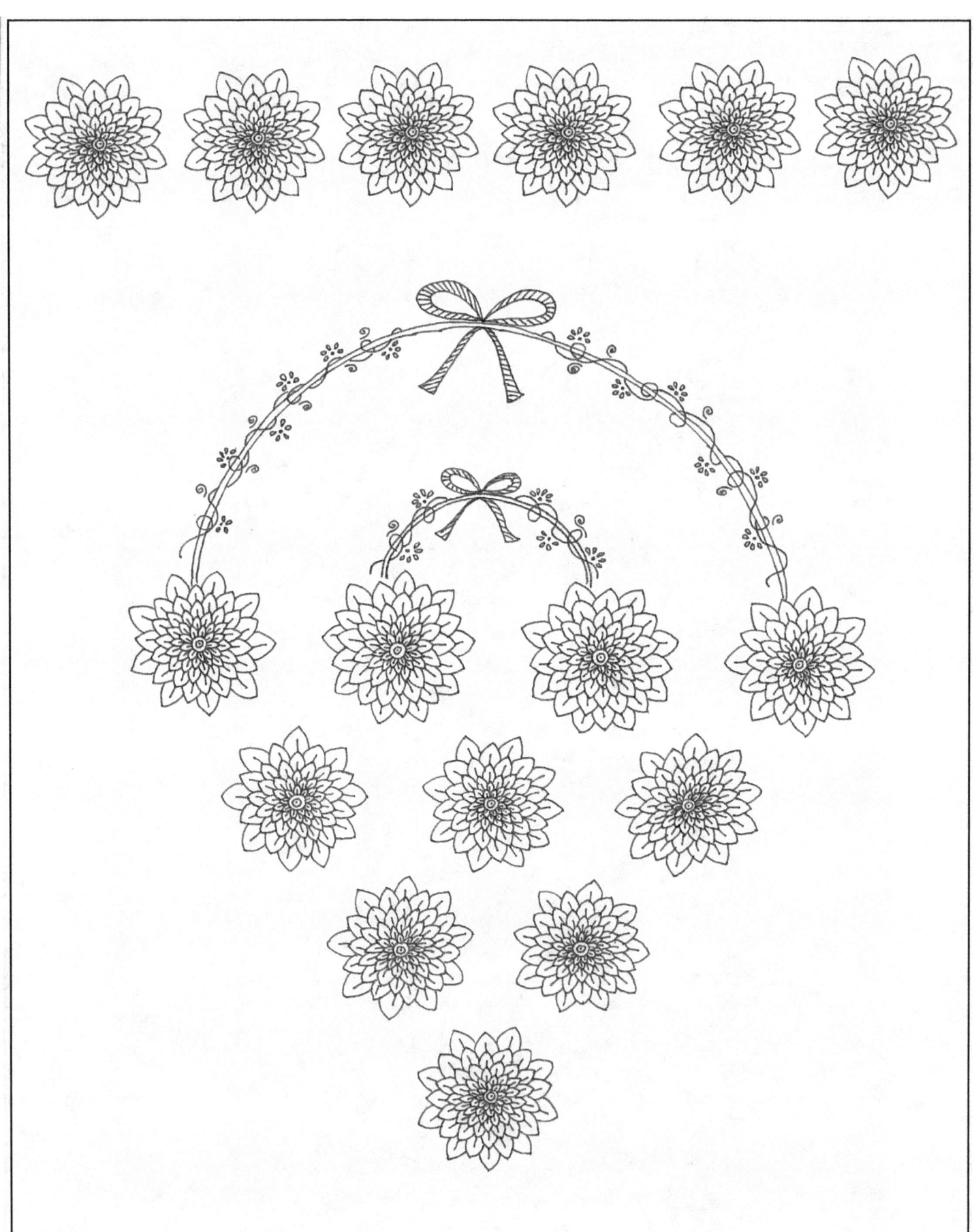

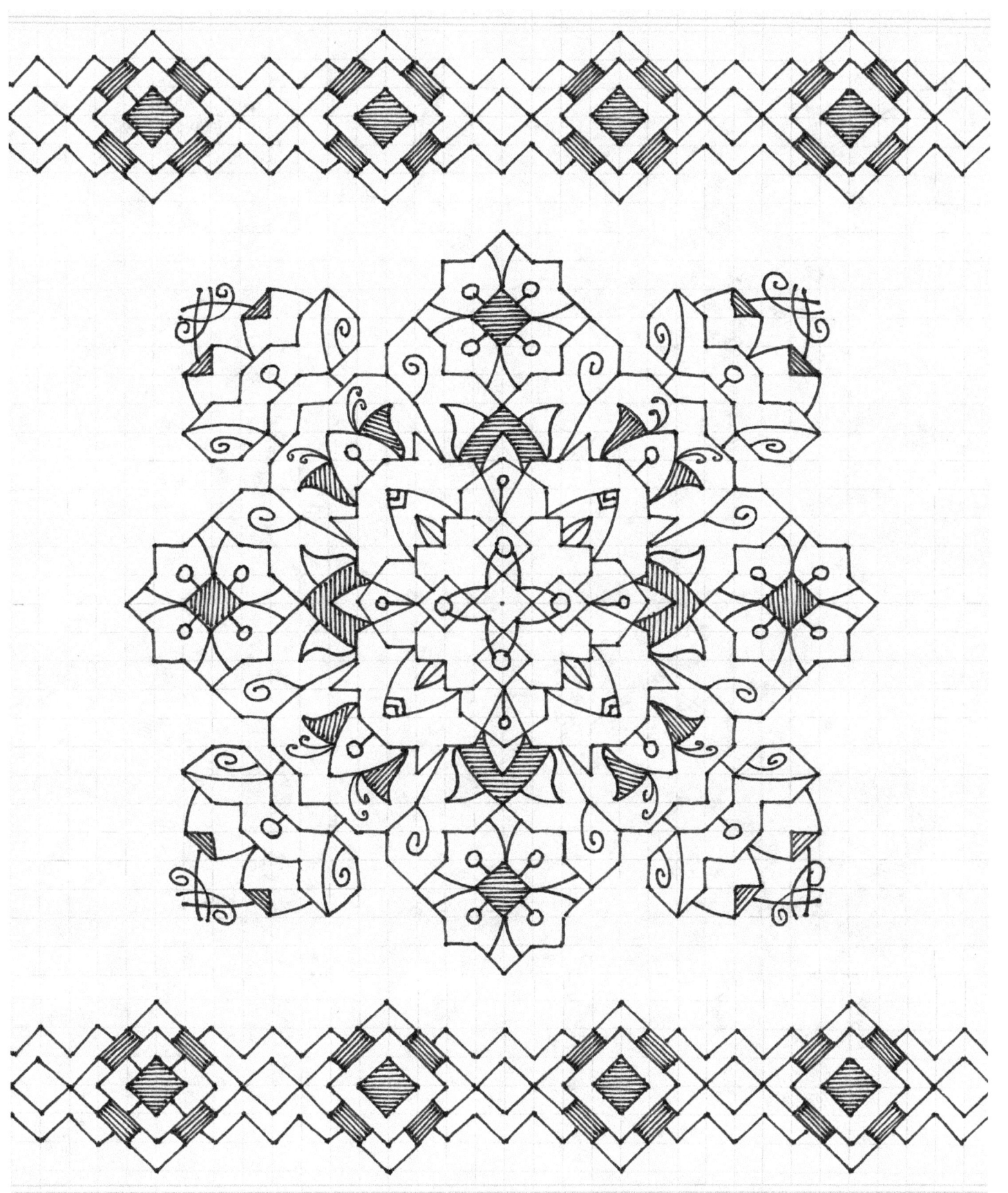

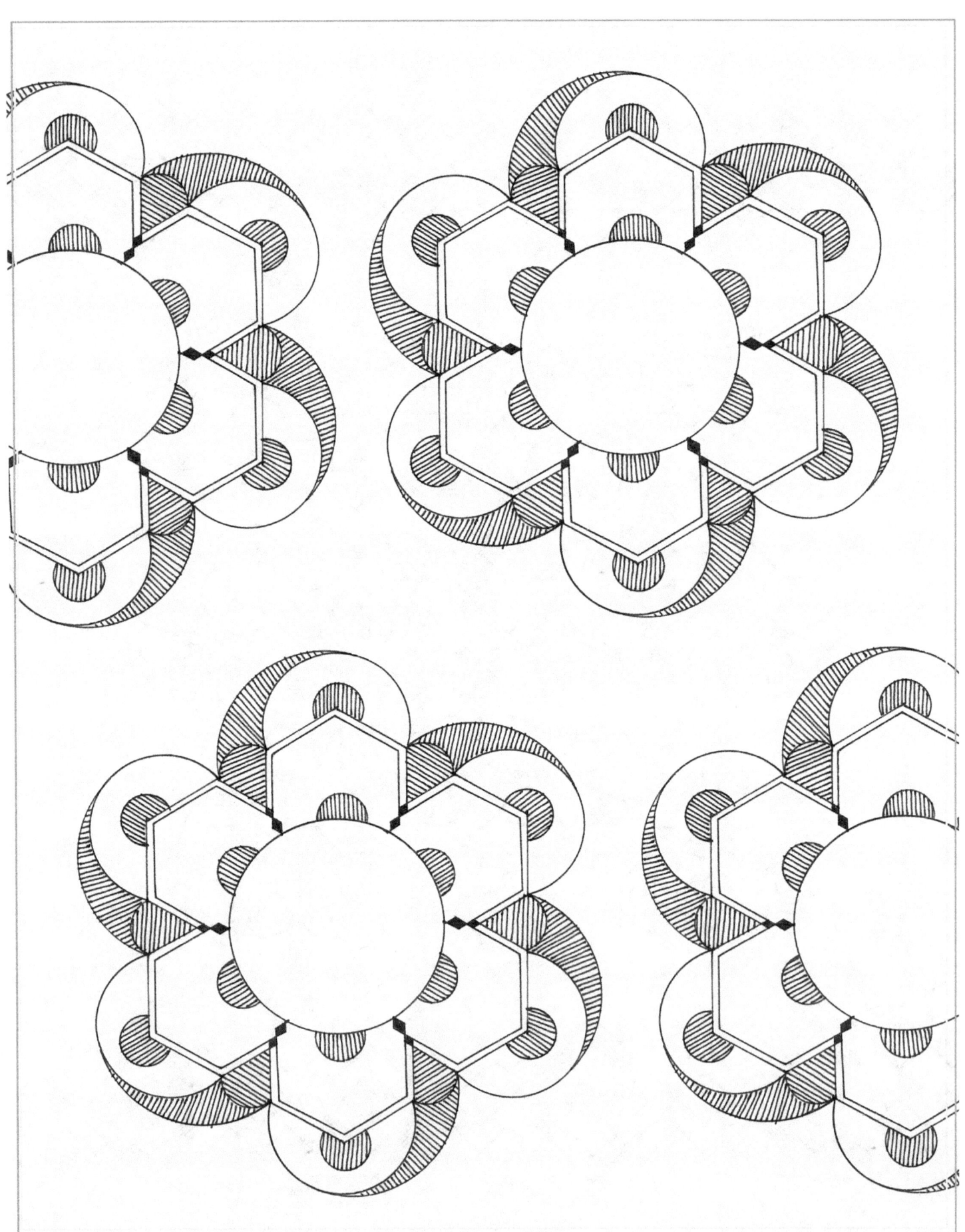

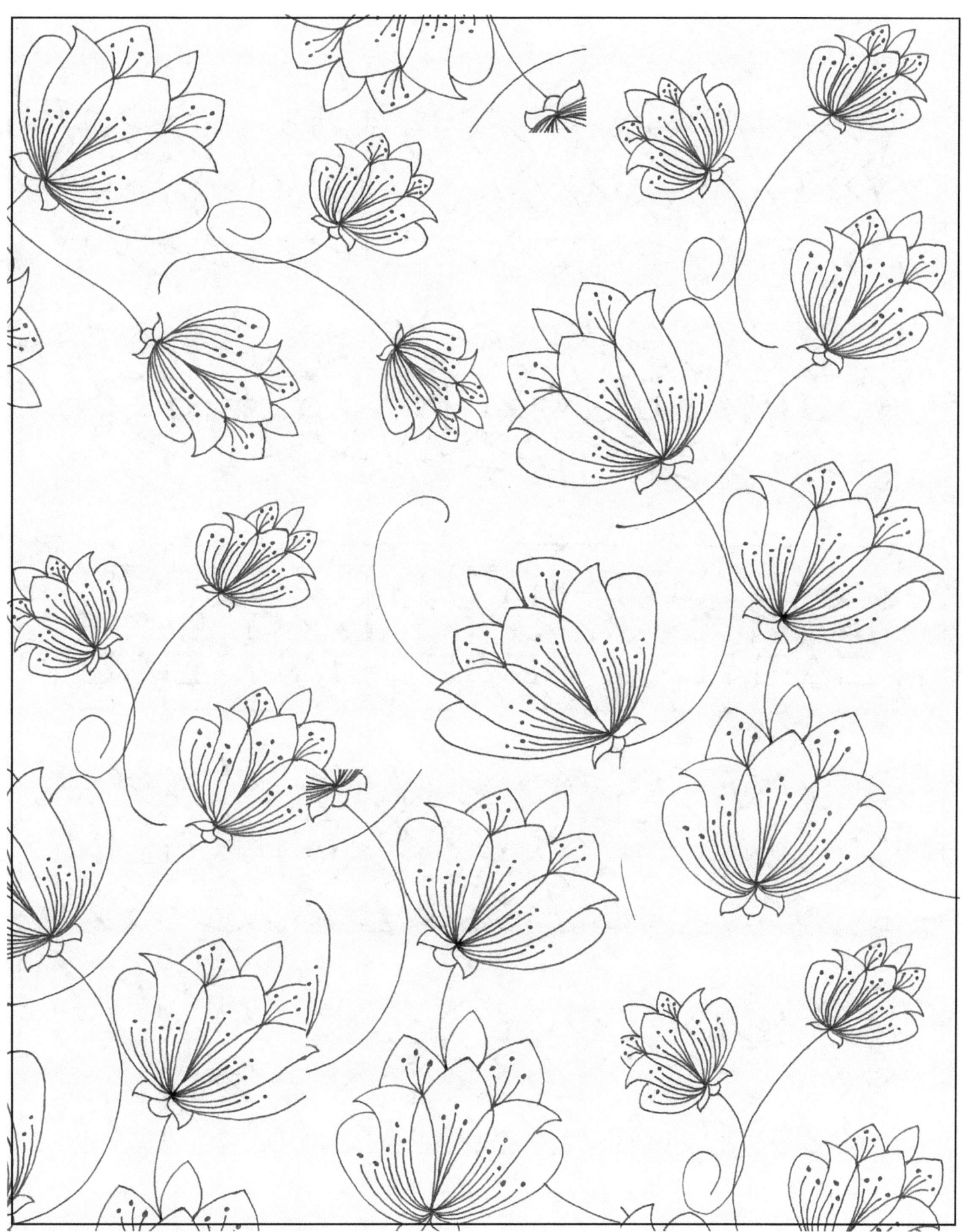

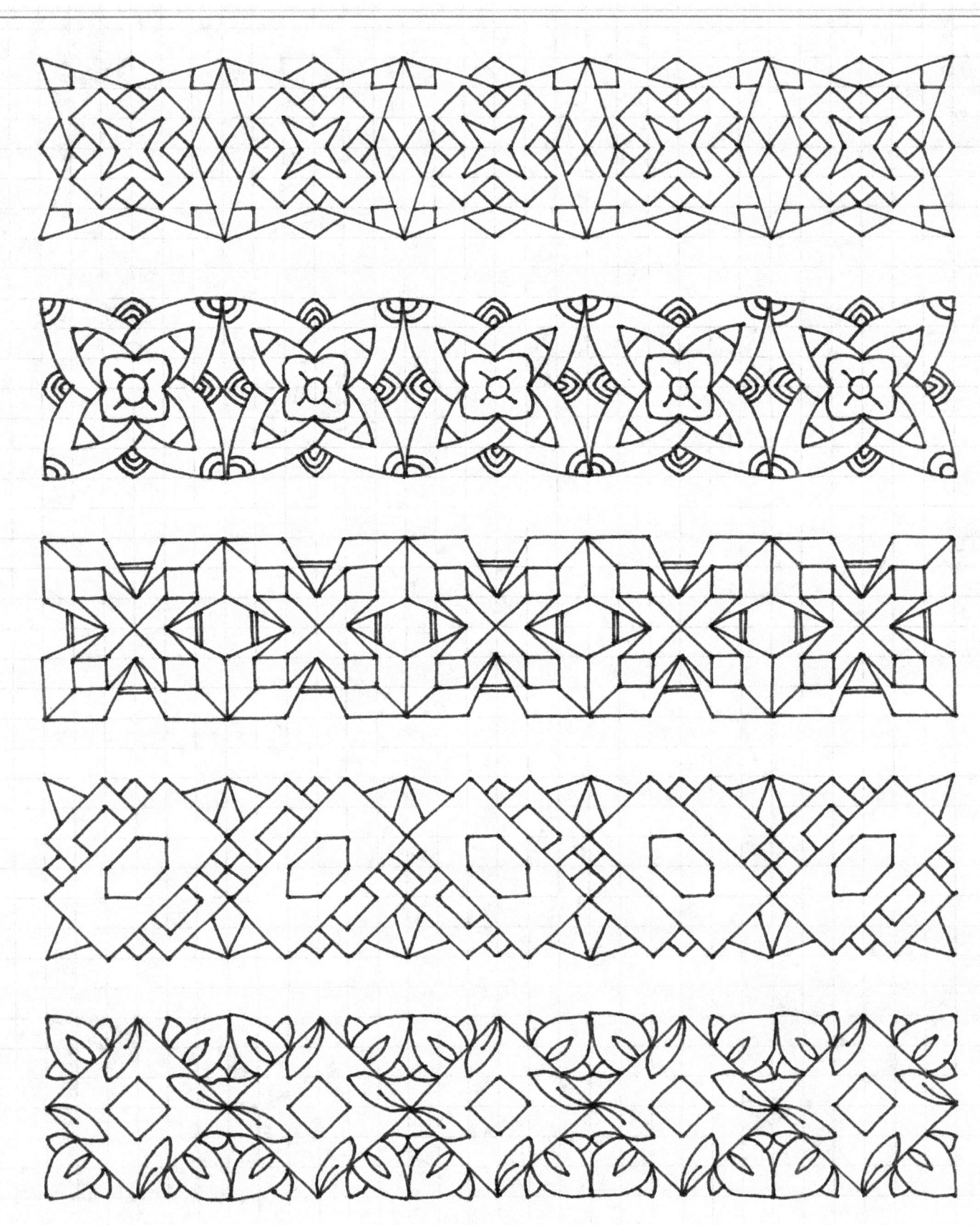

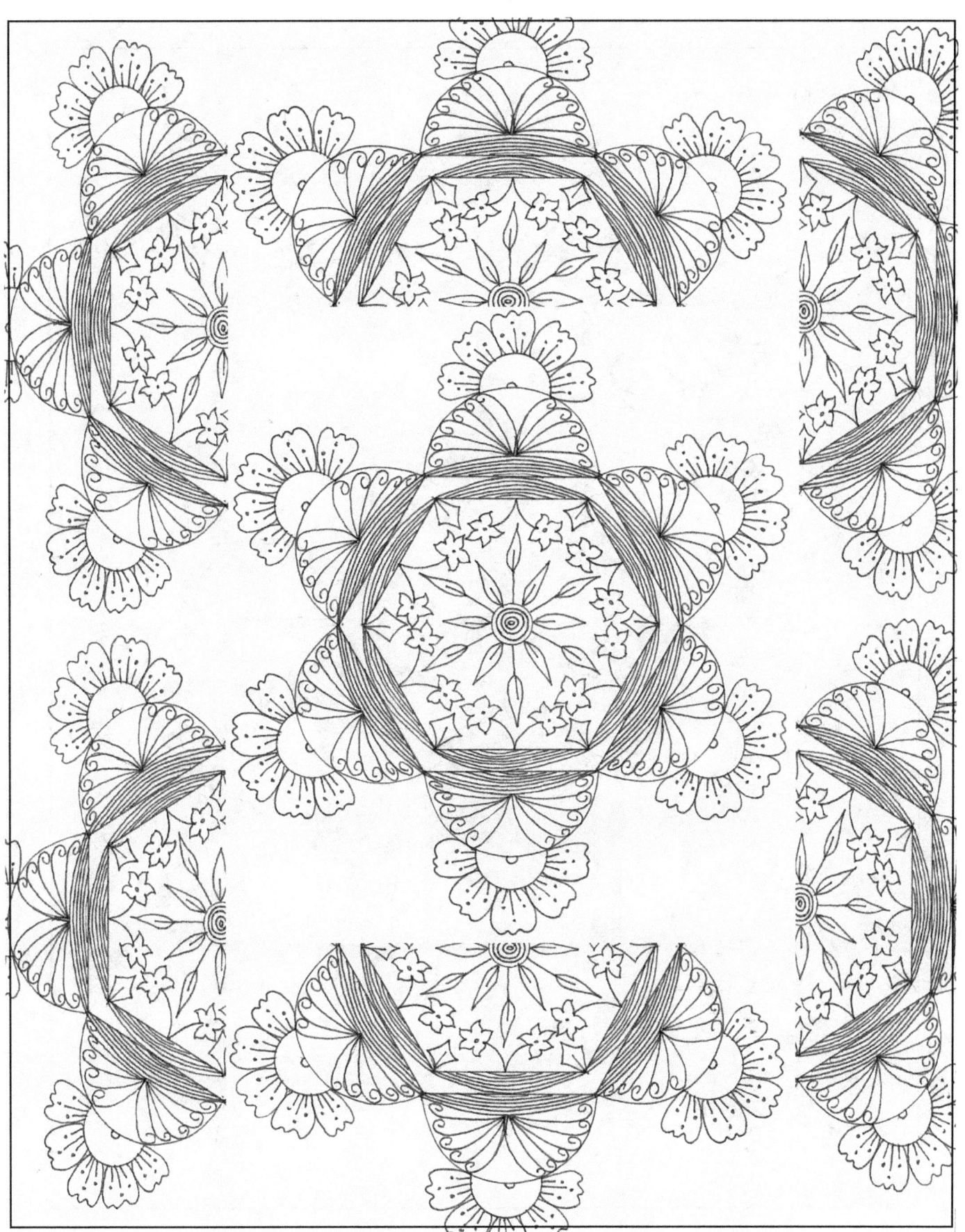

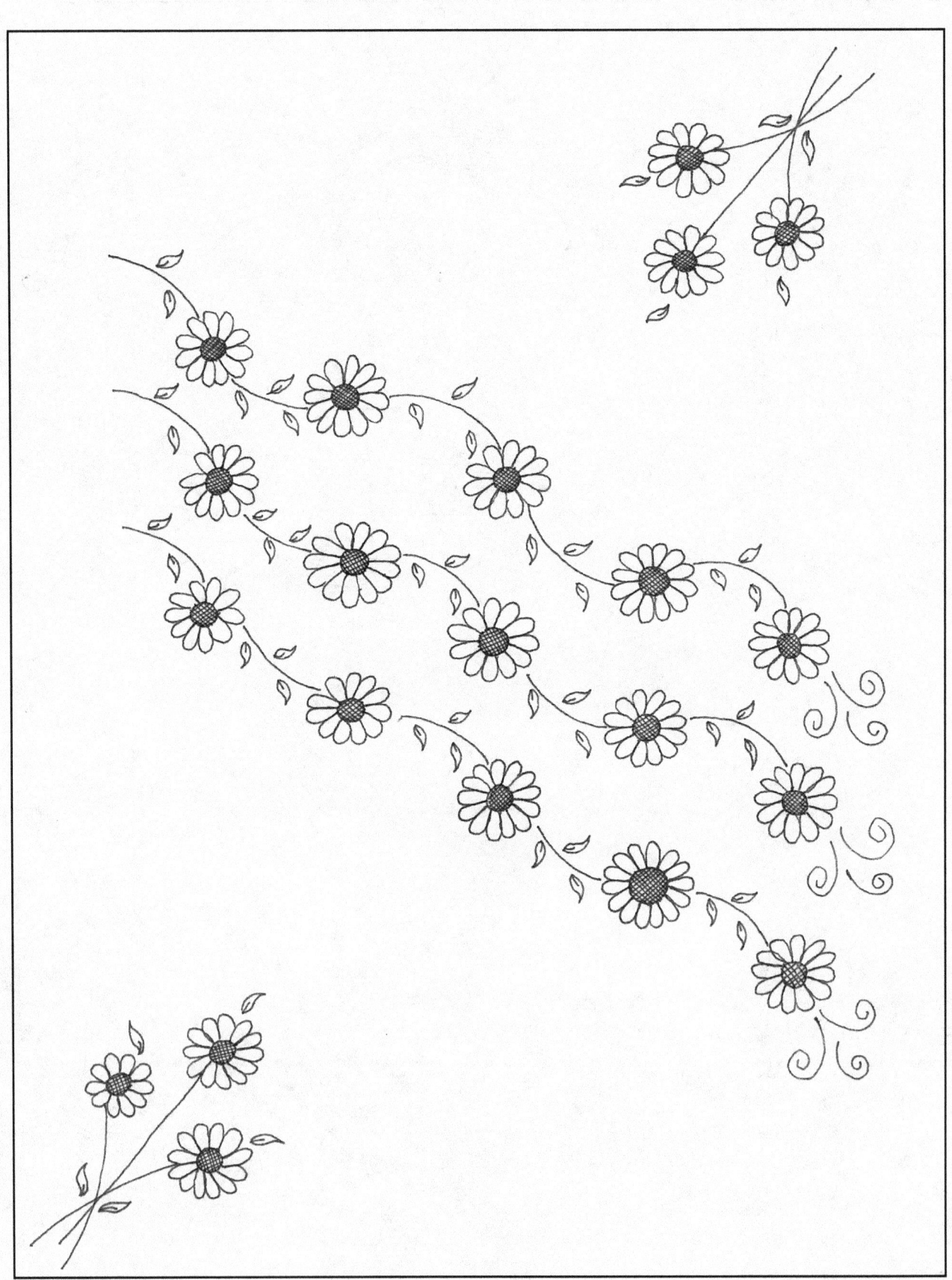

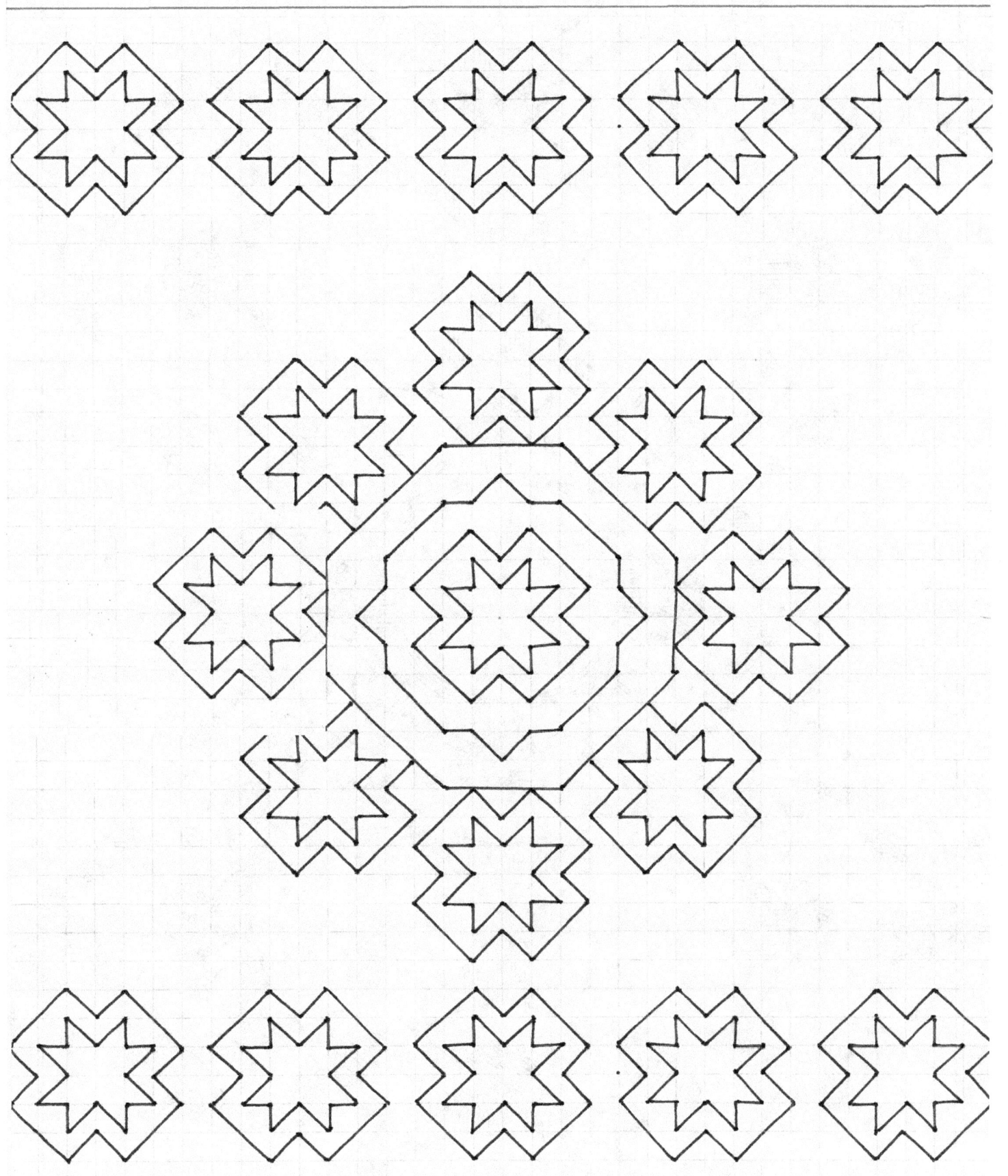

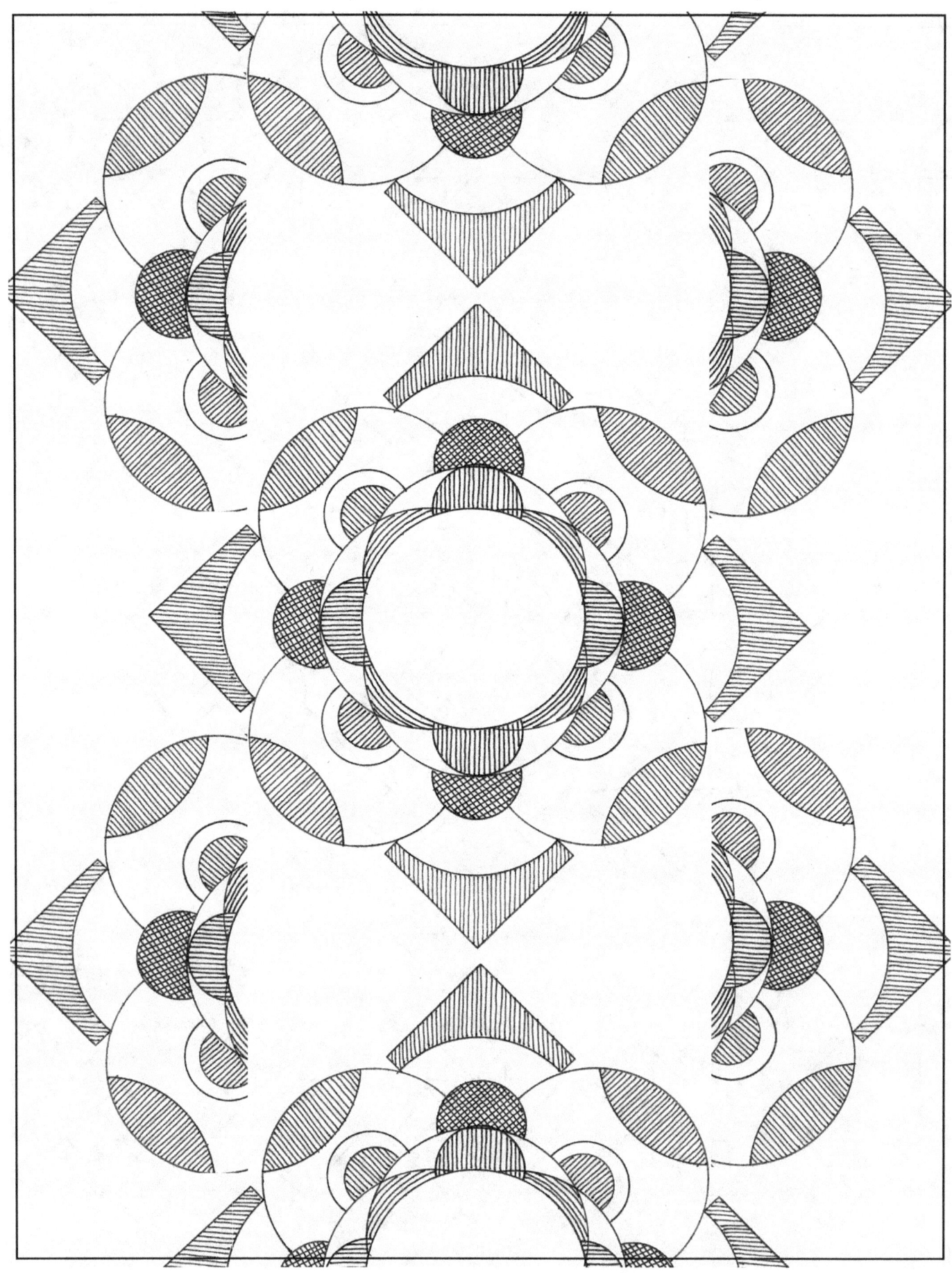

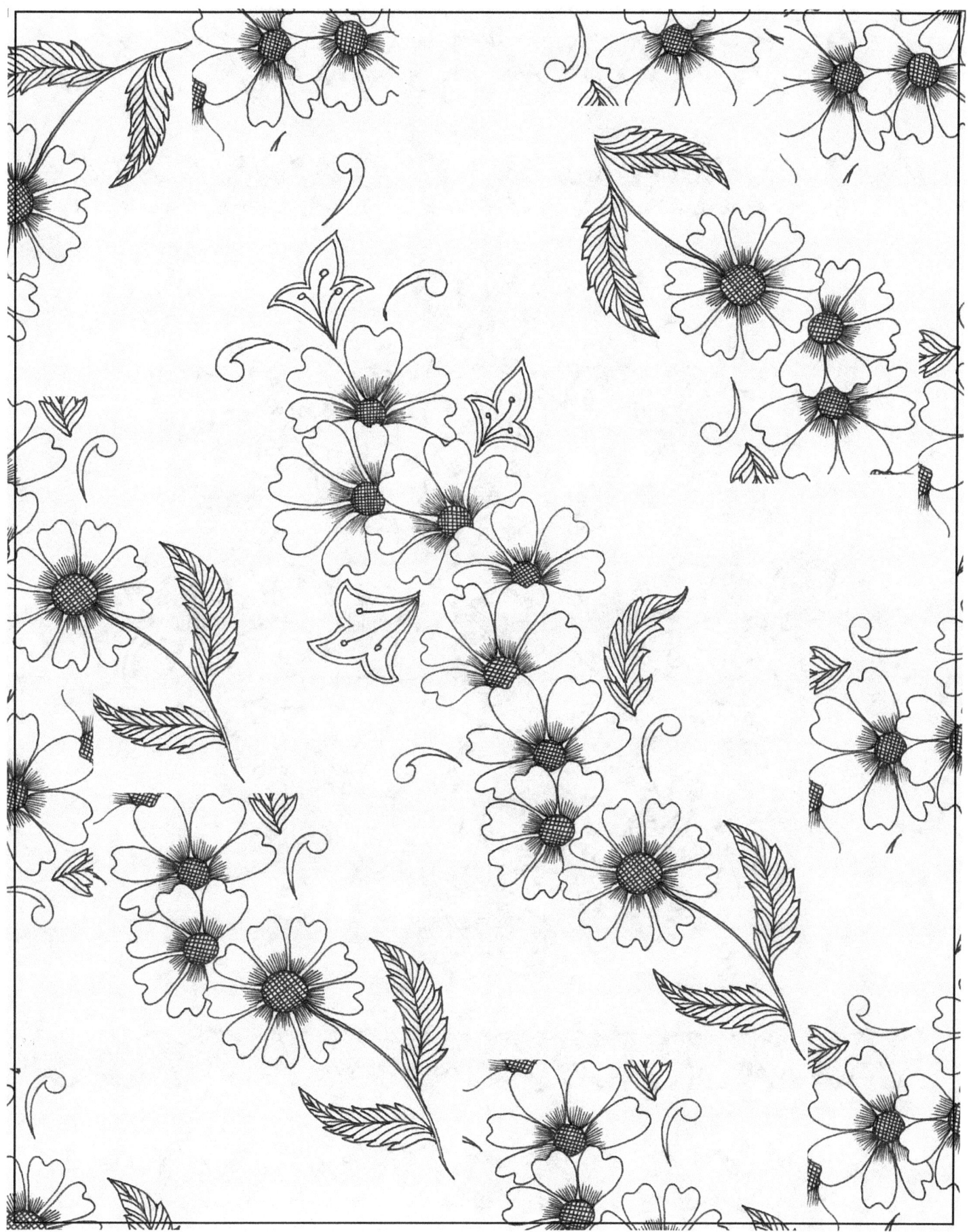

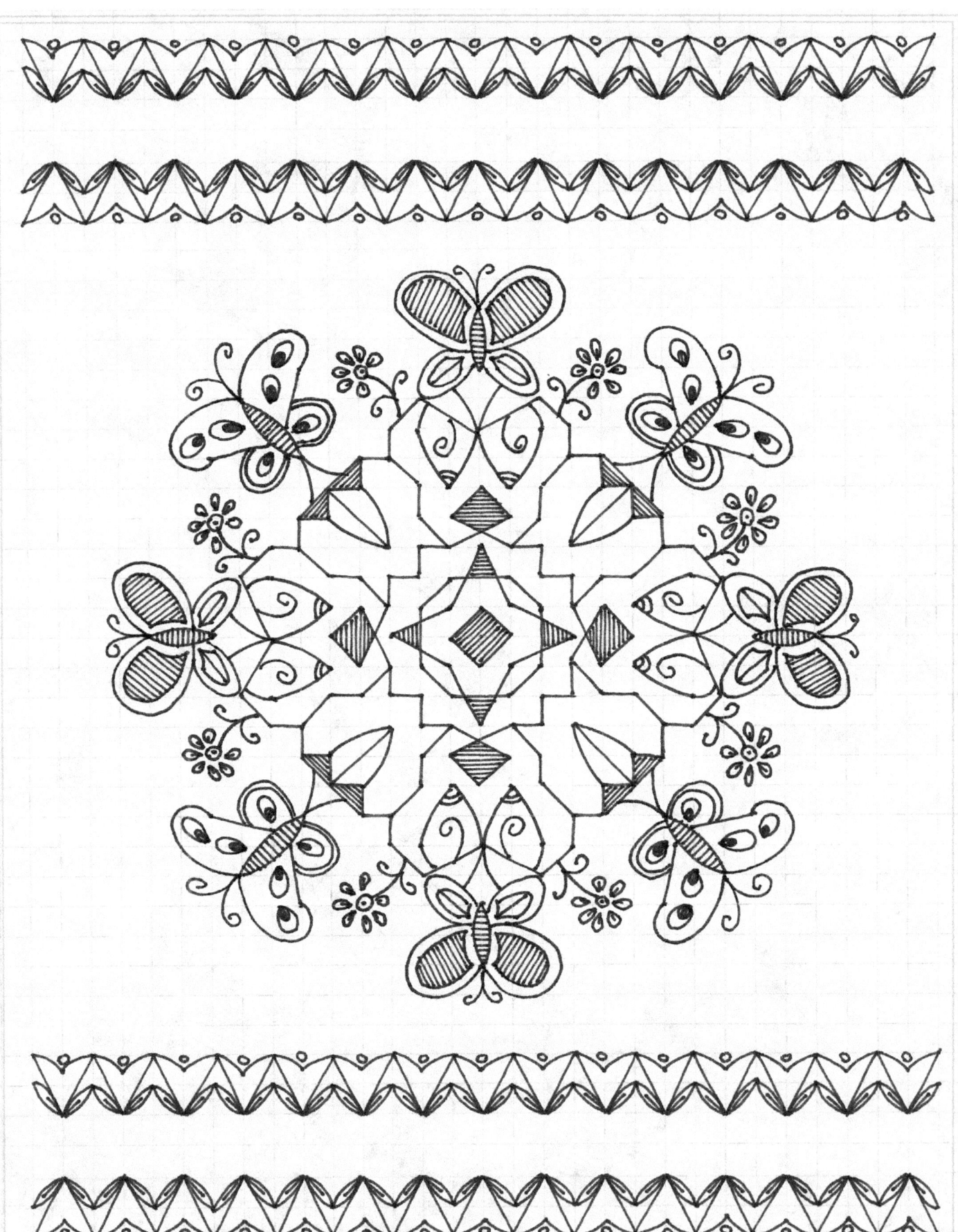

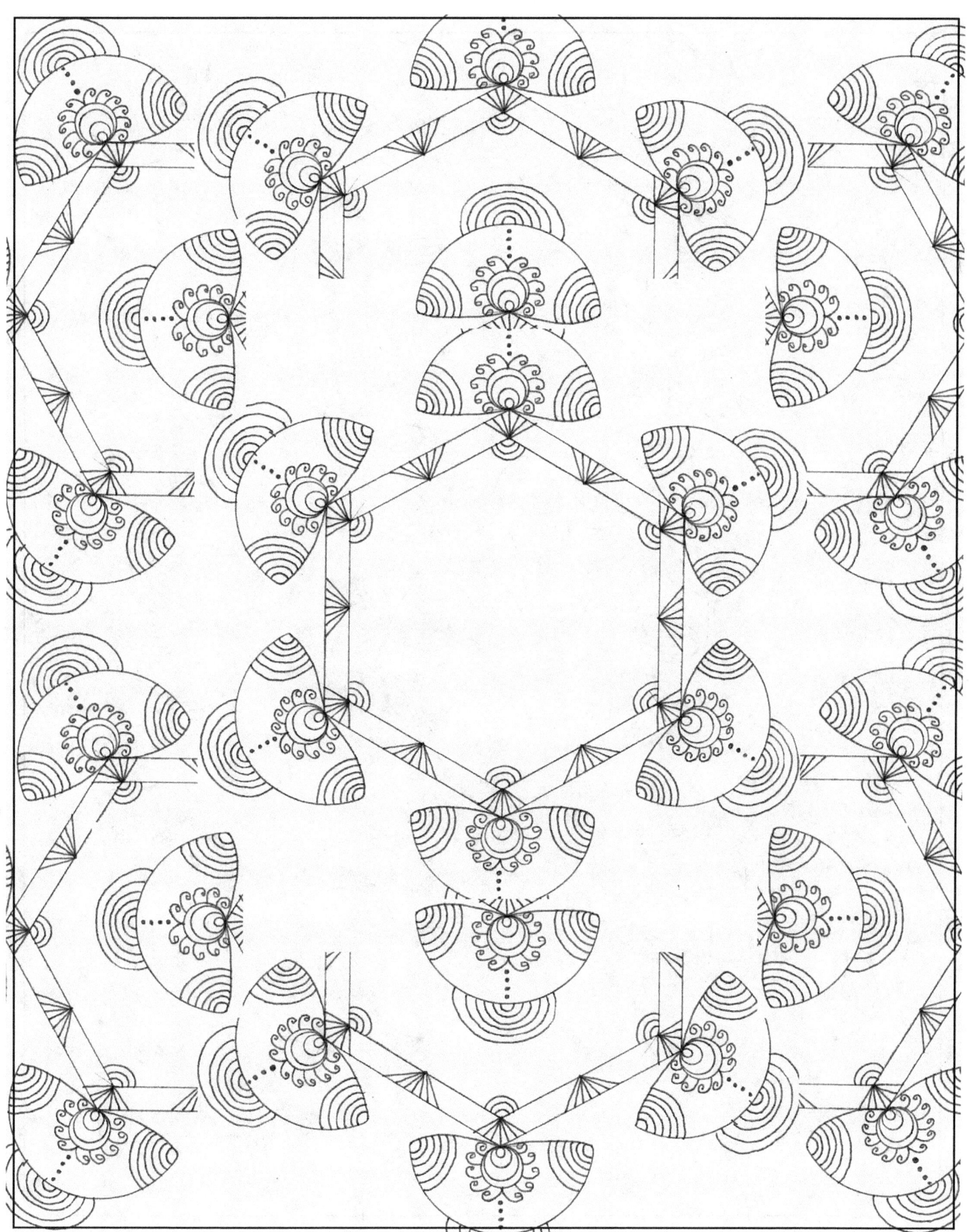

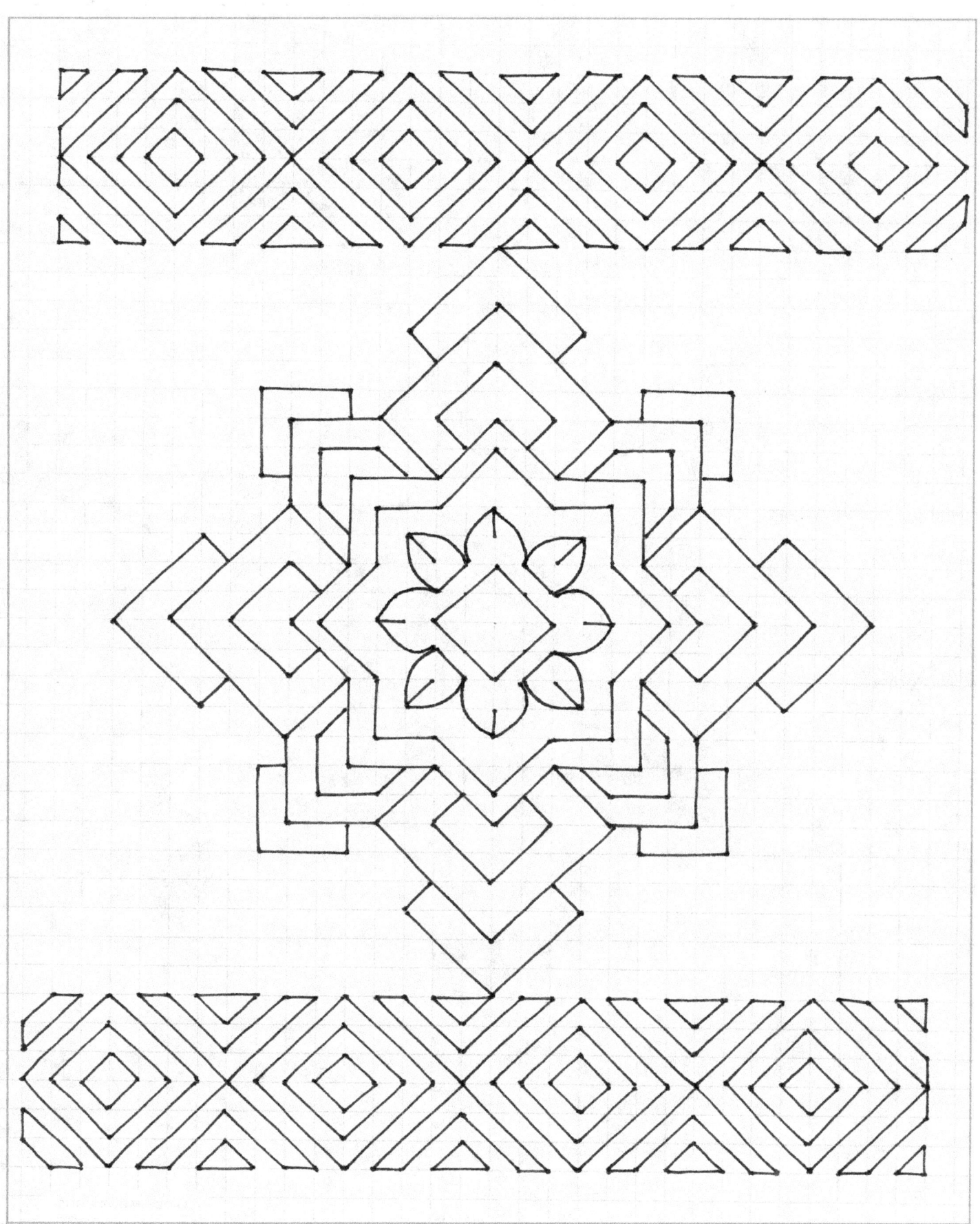

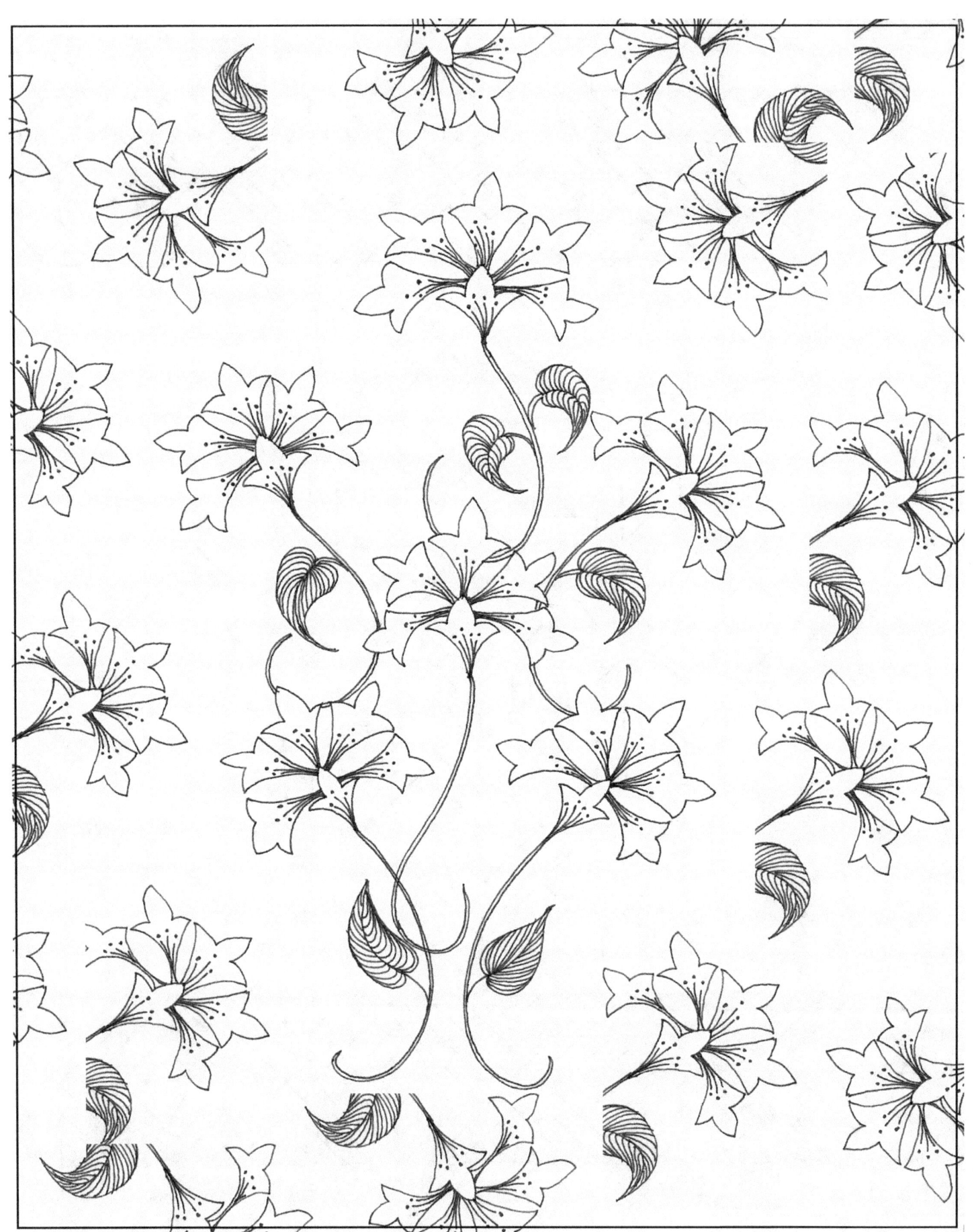

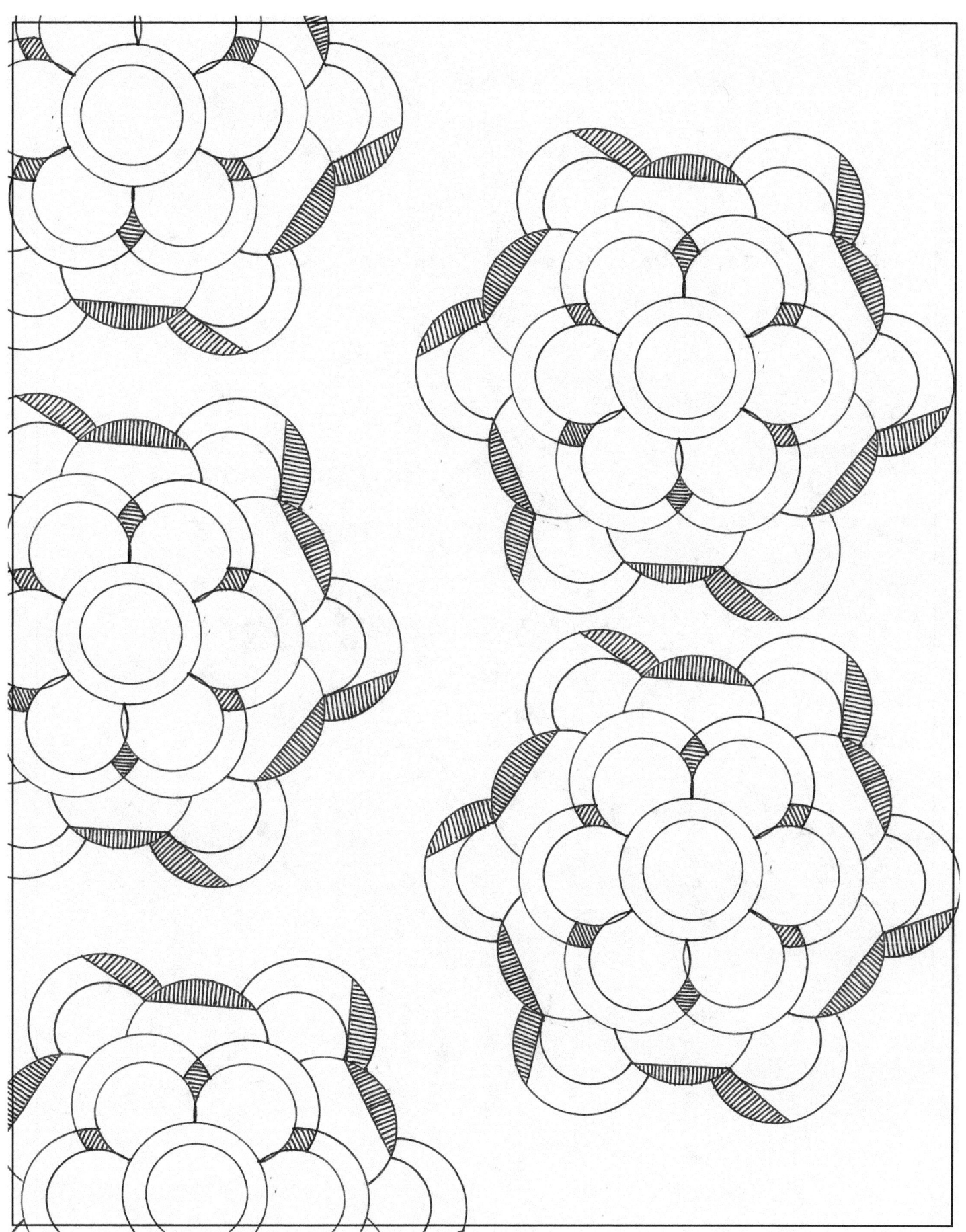

37

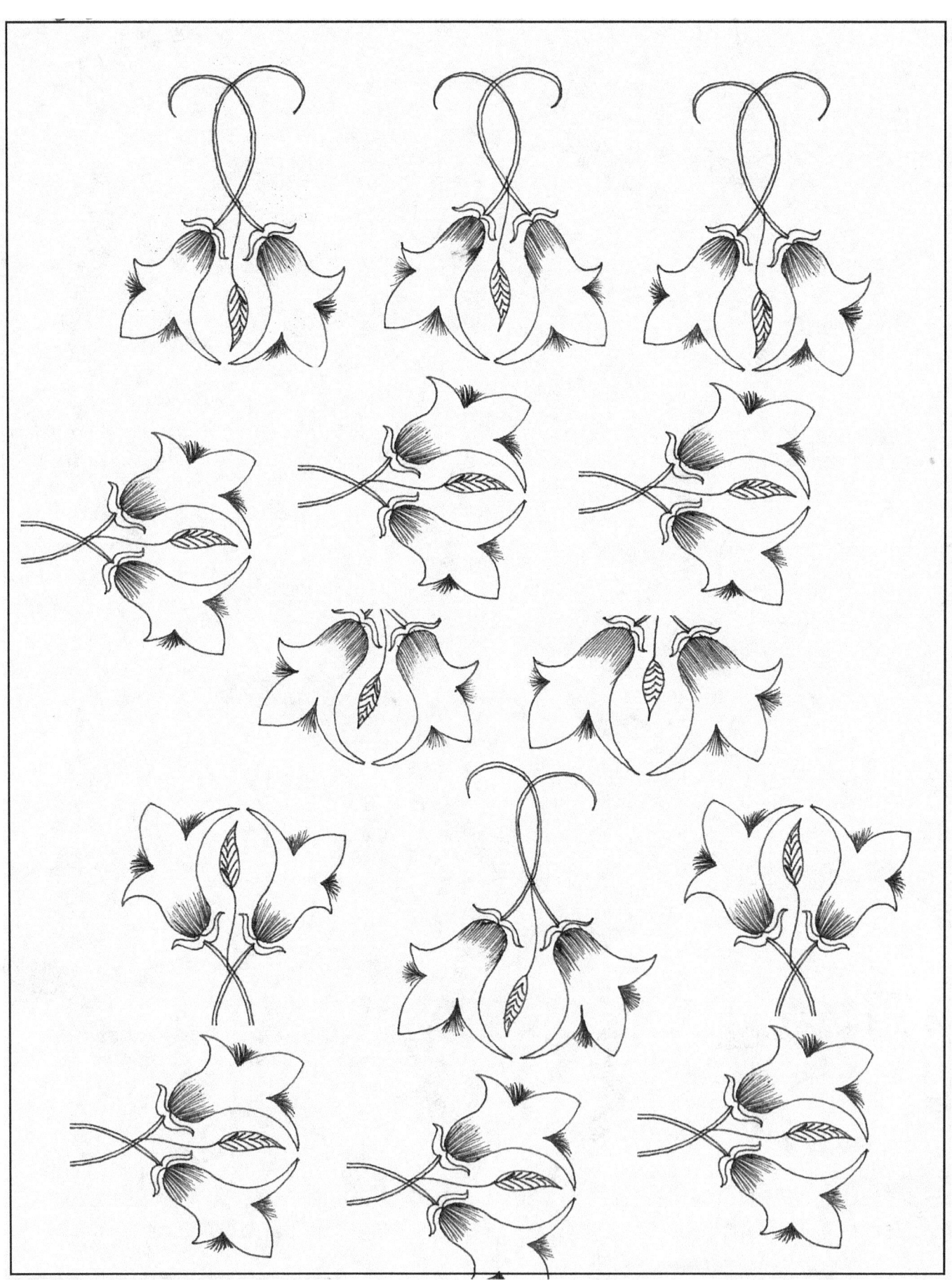

38

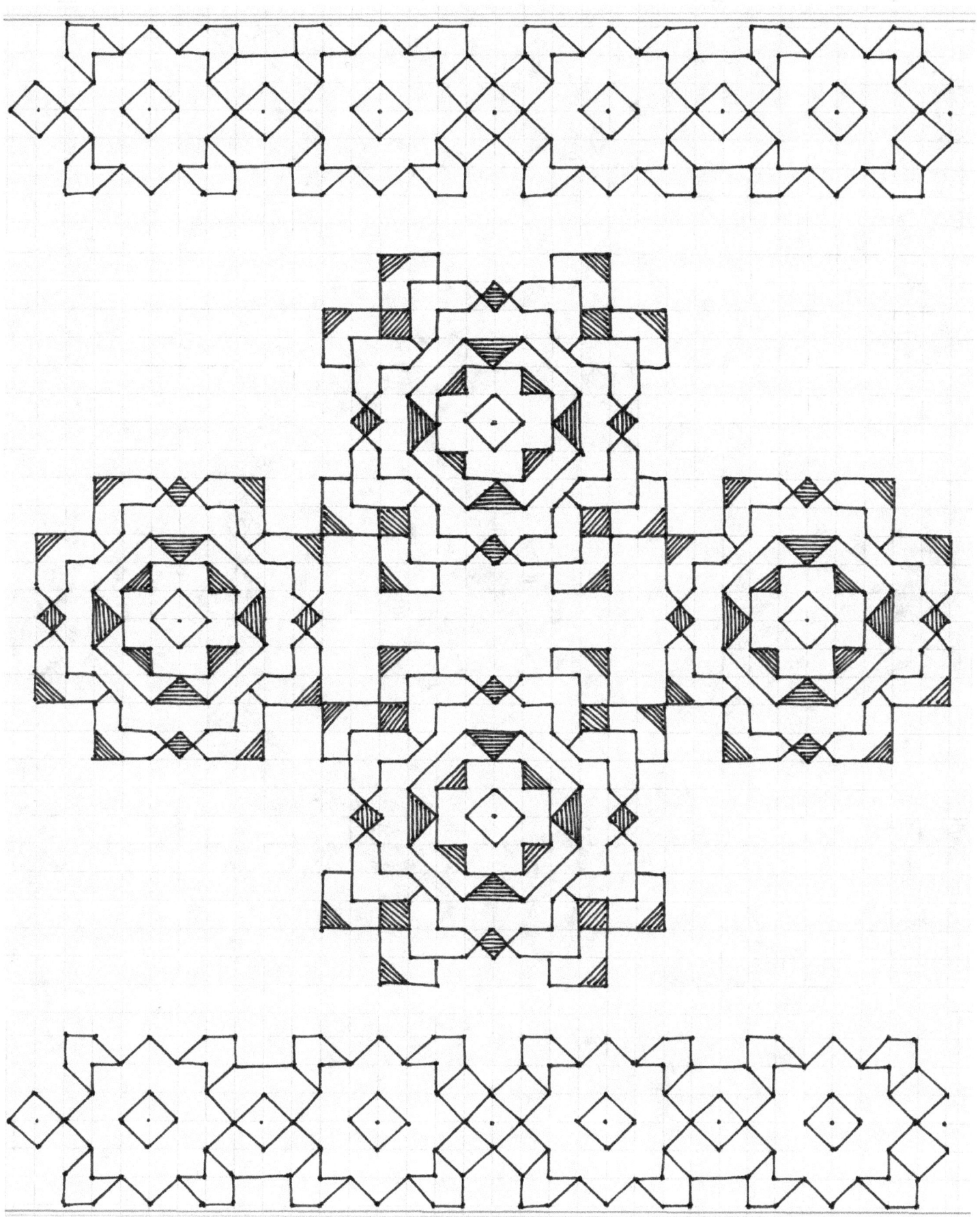

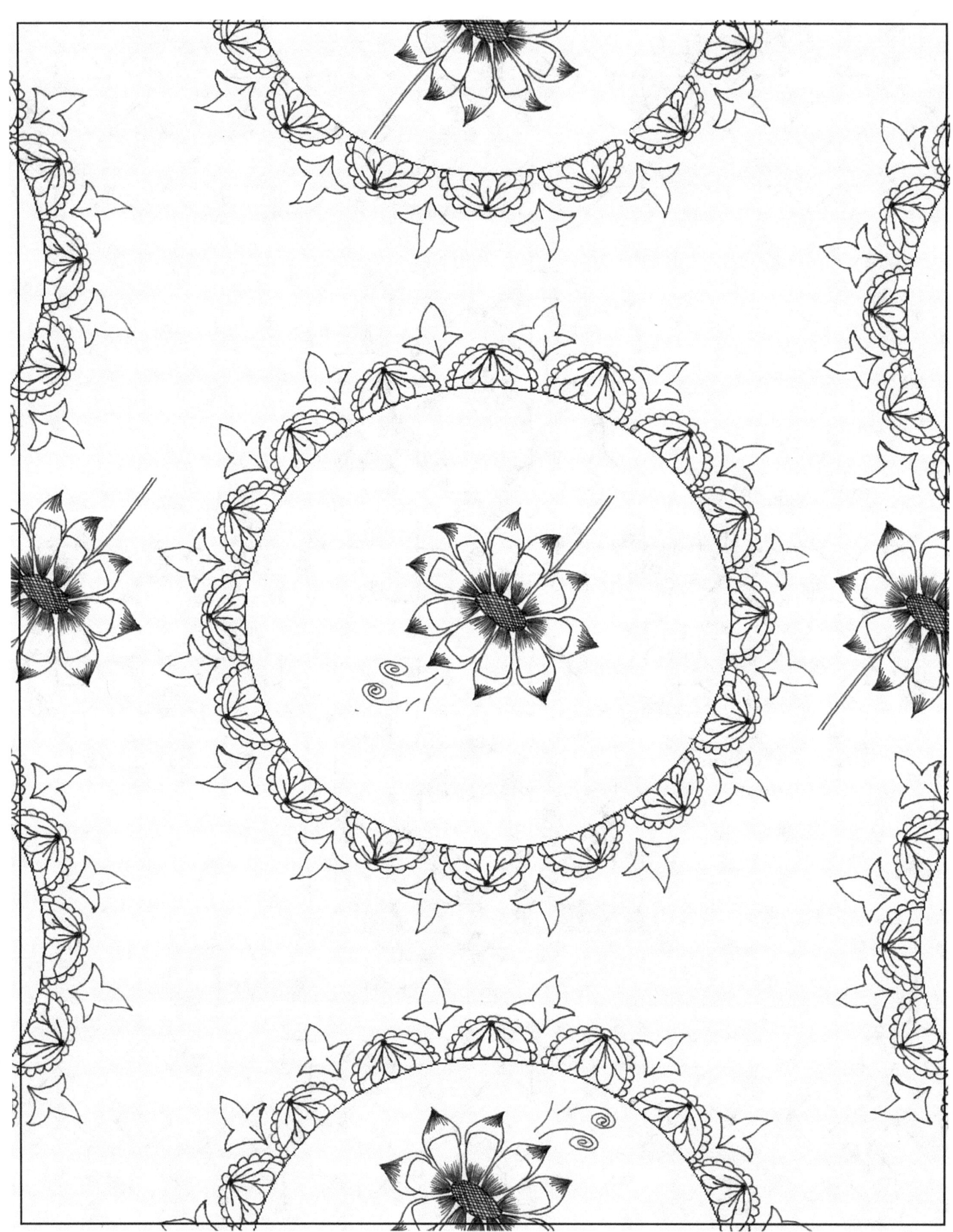

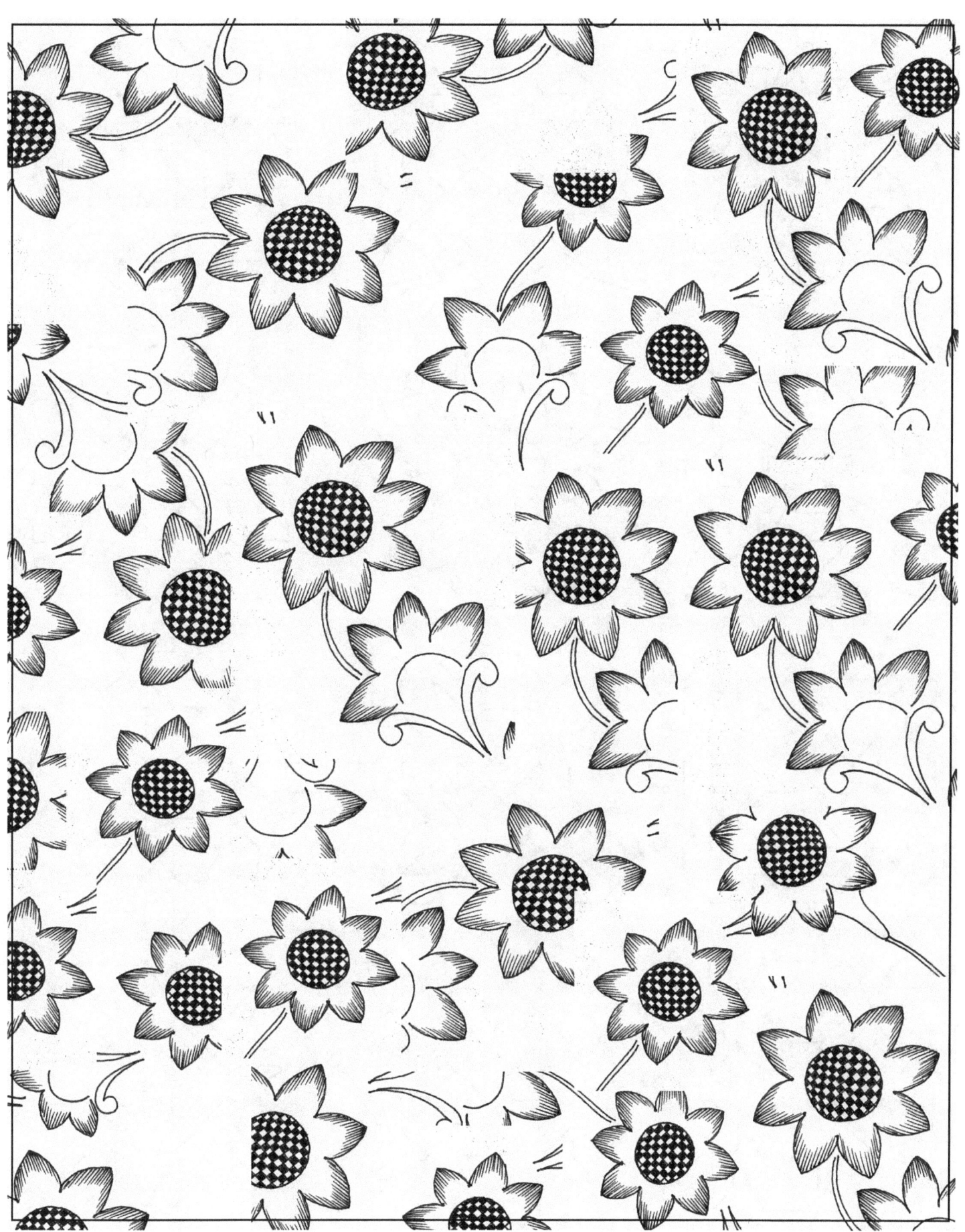

41

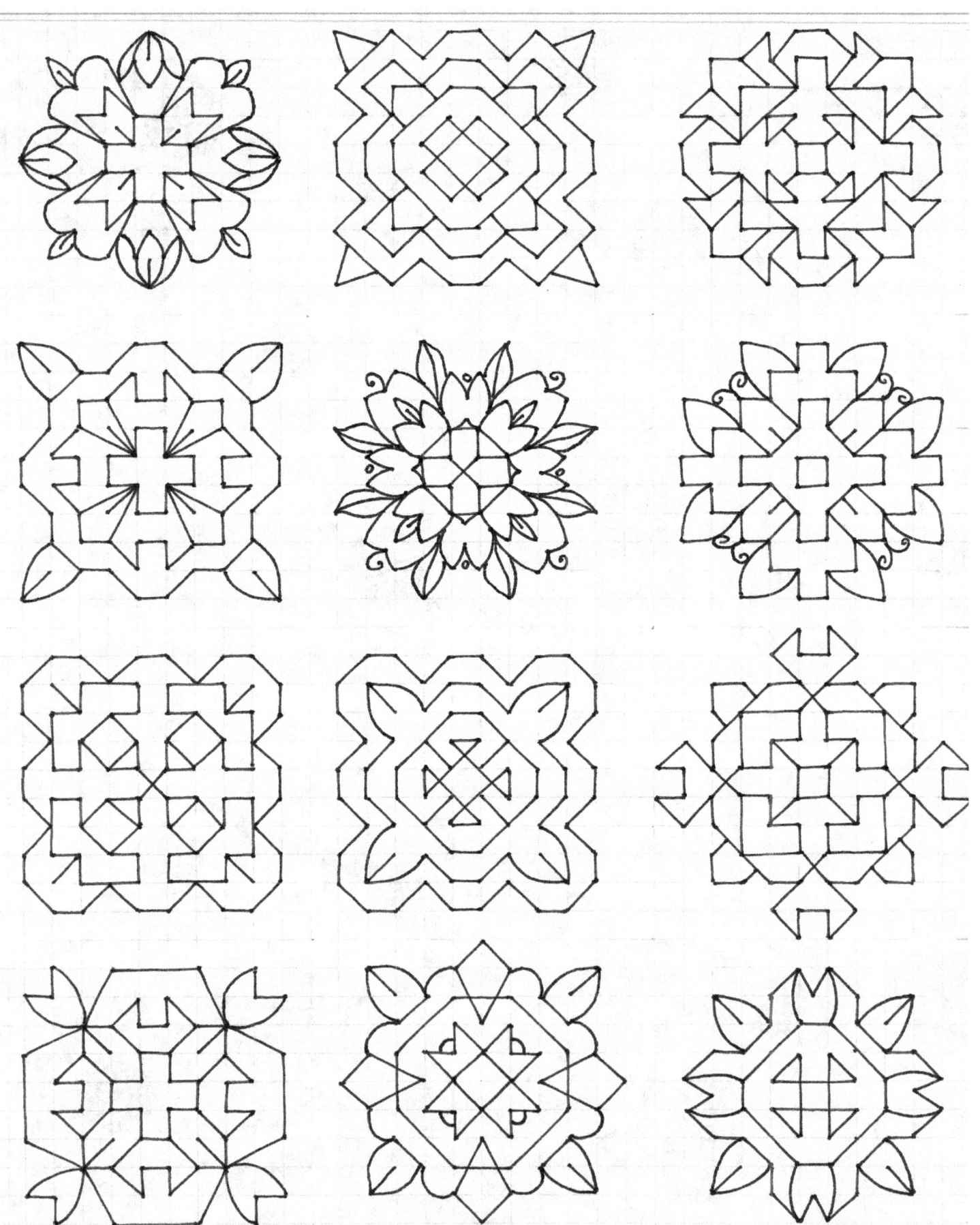

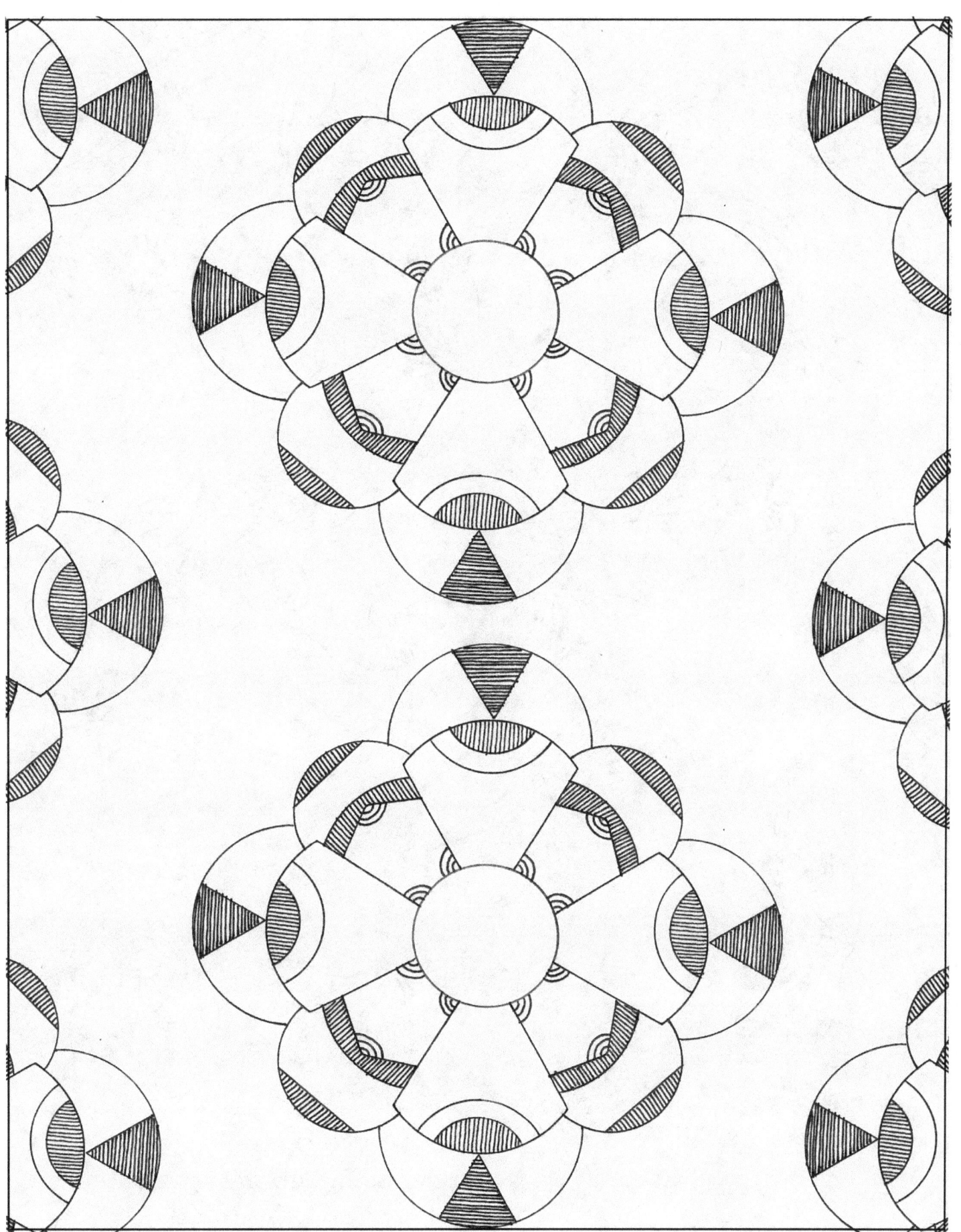

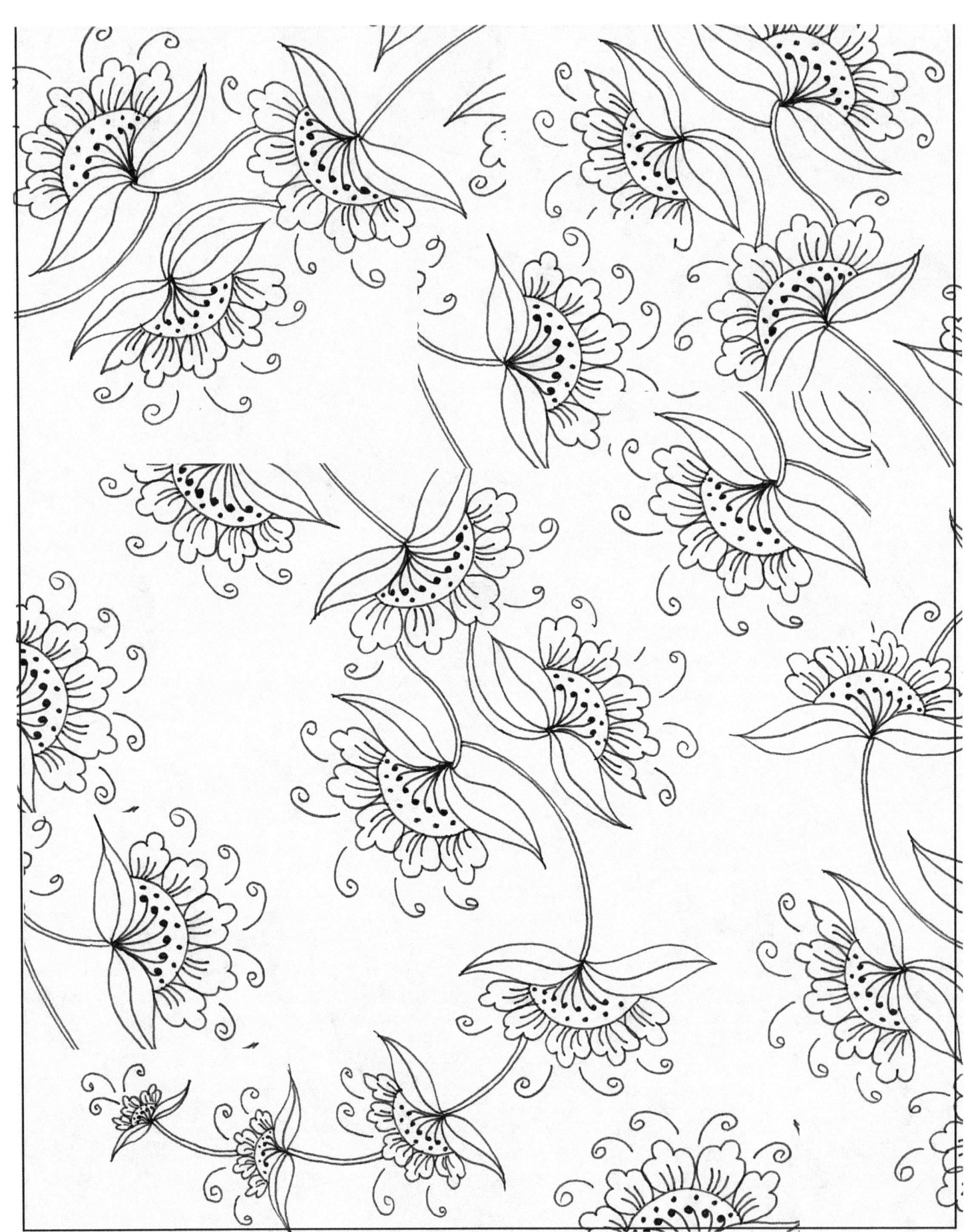

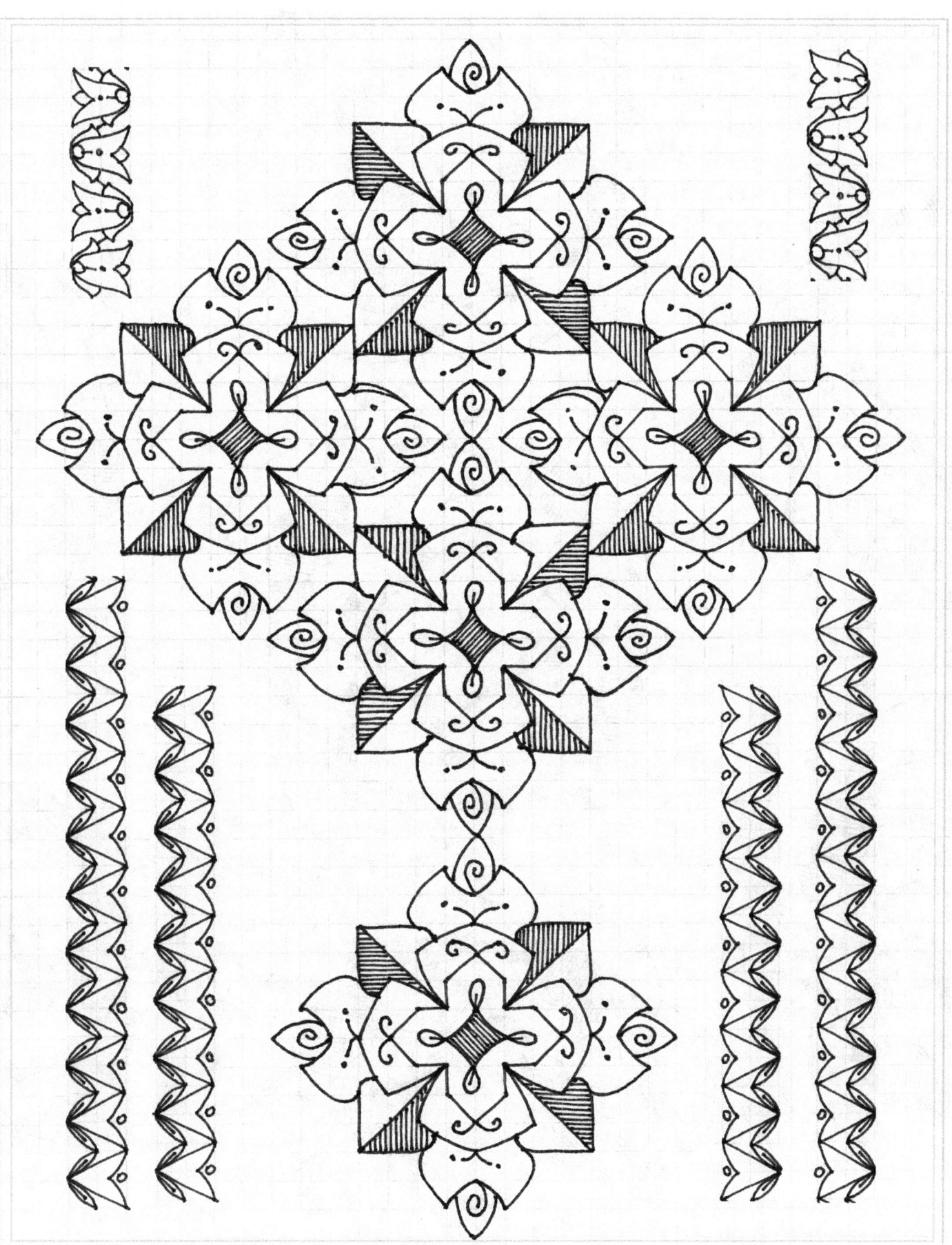

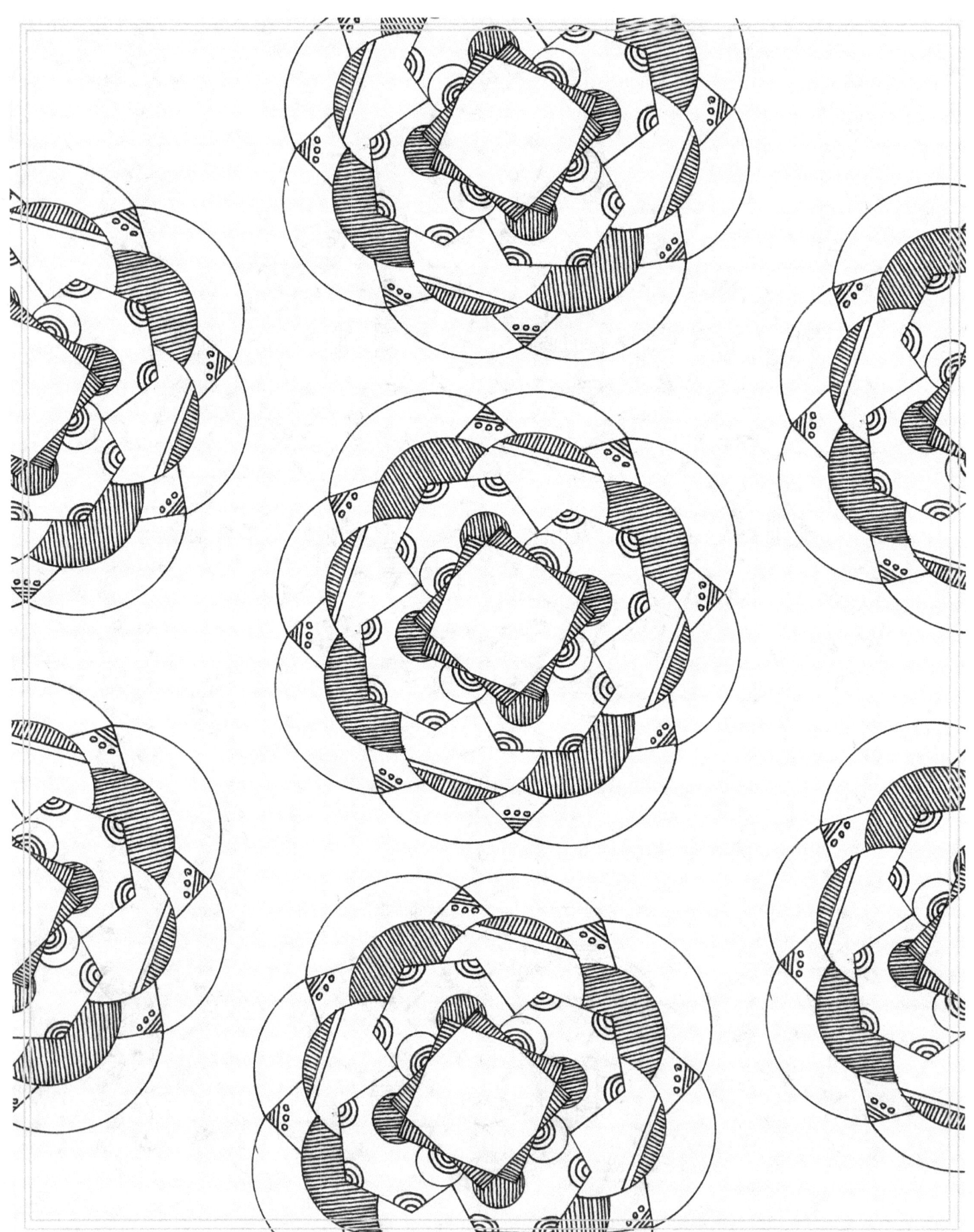

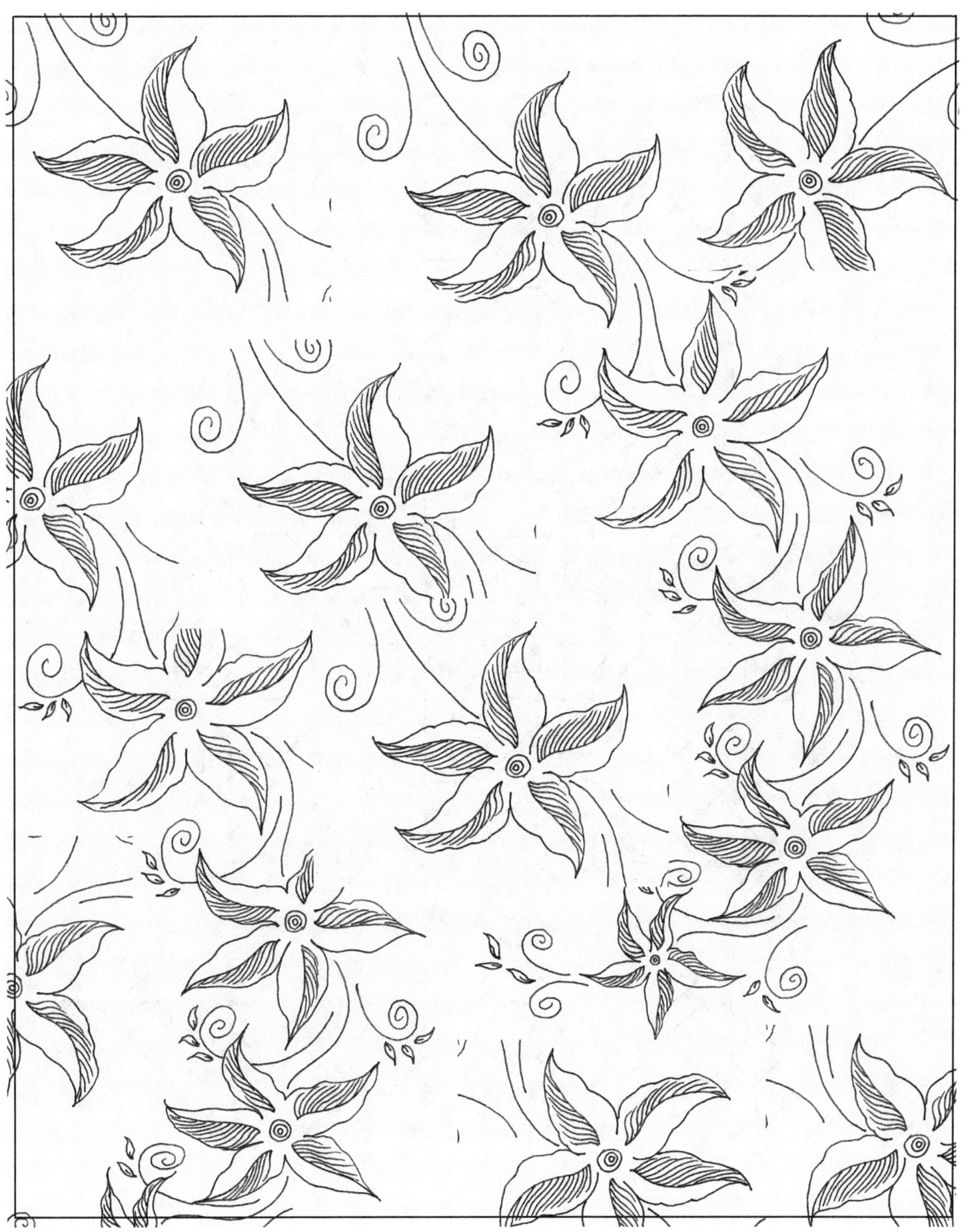

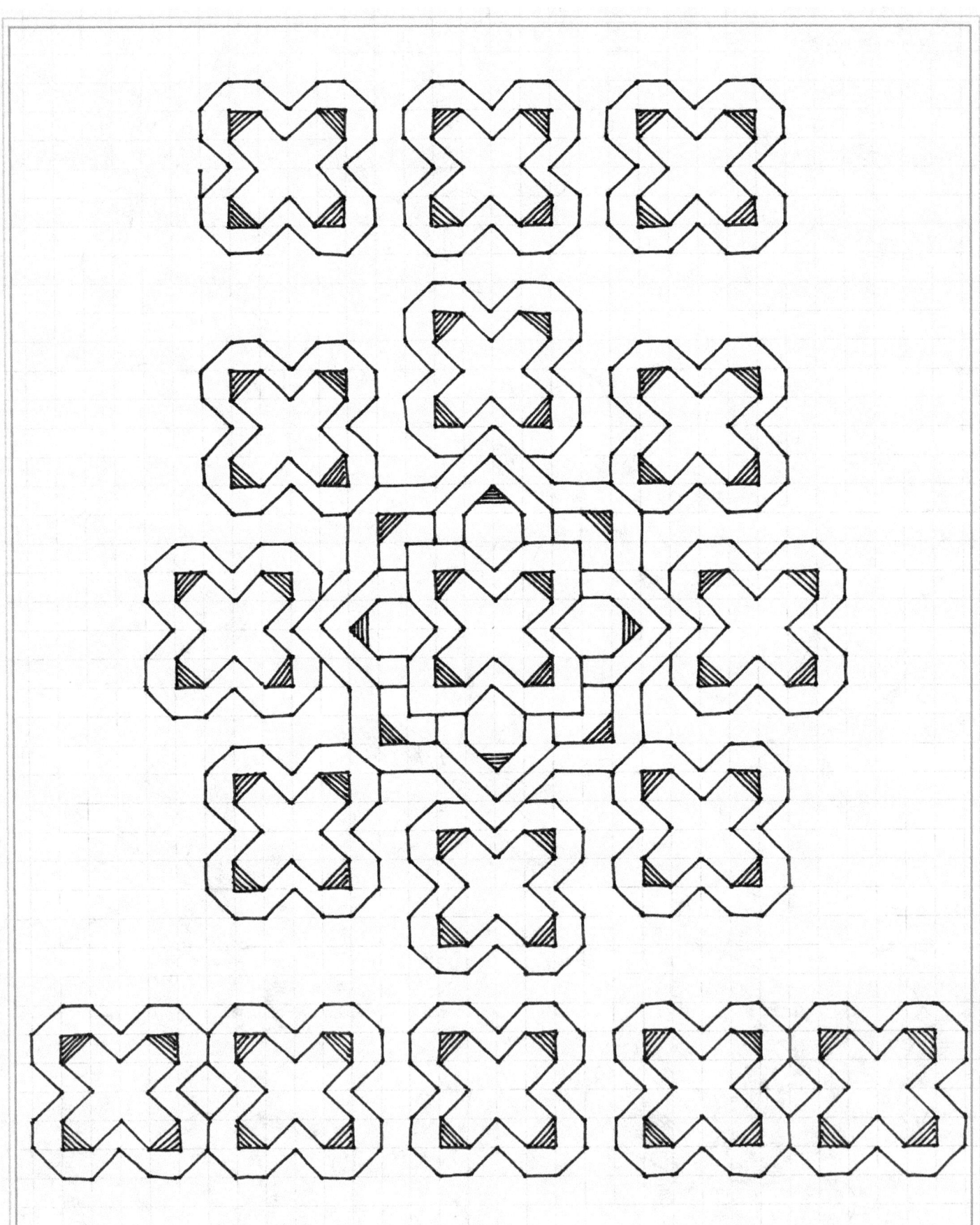

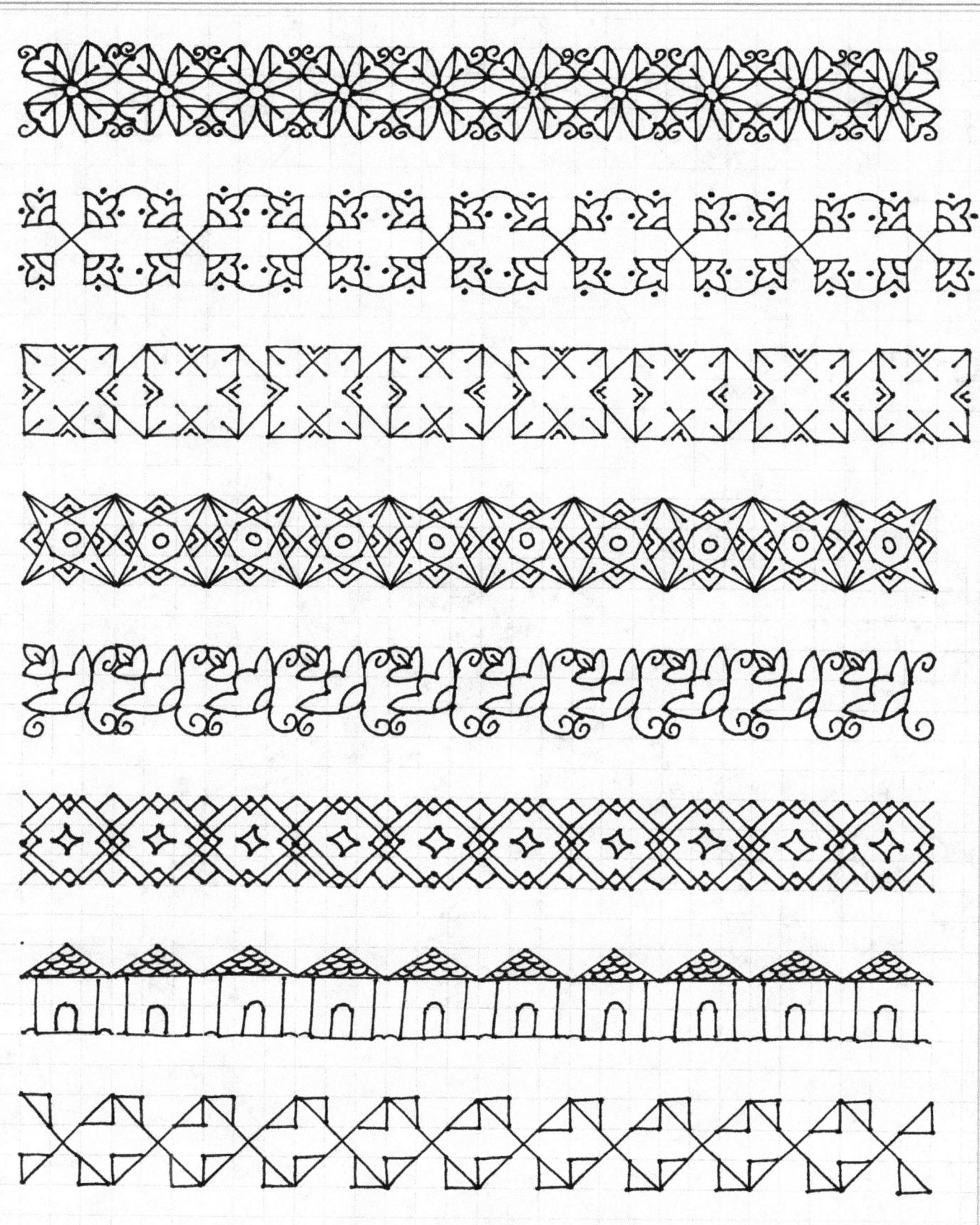

49

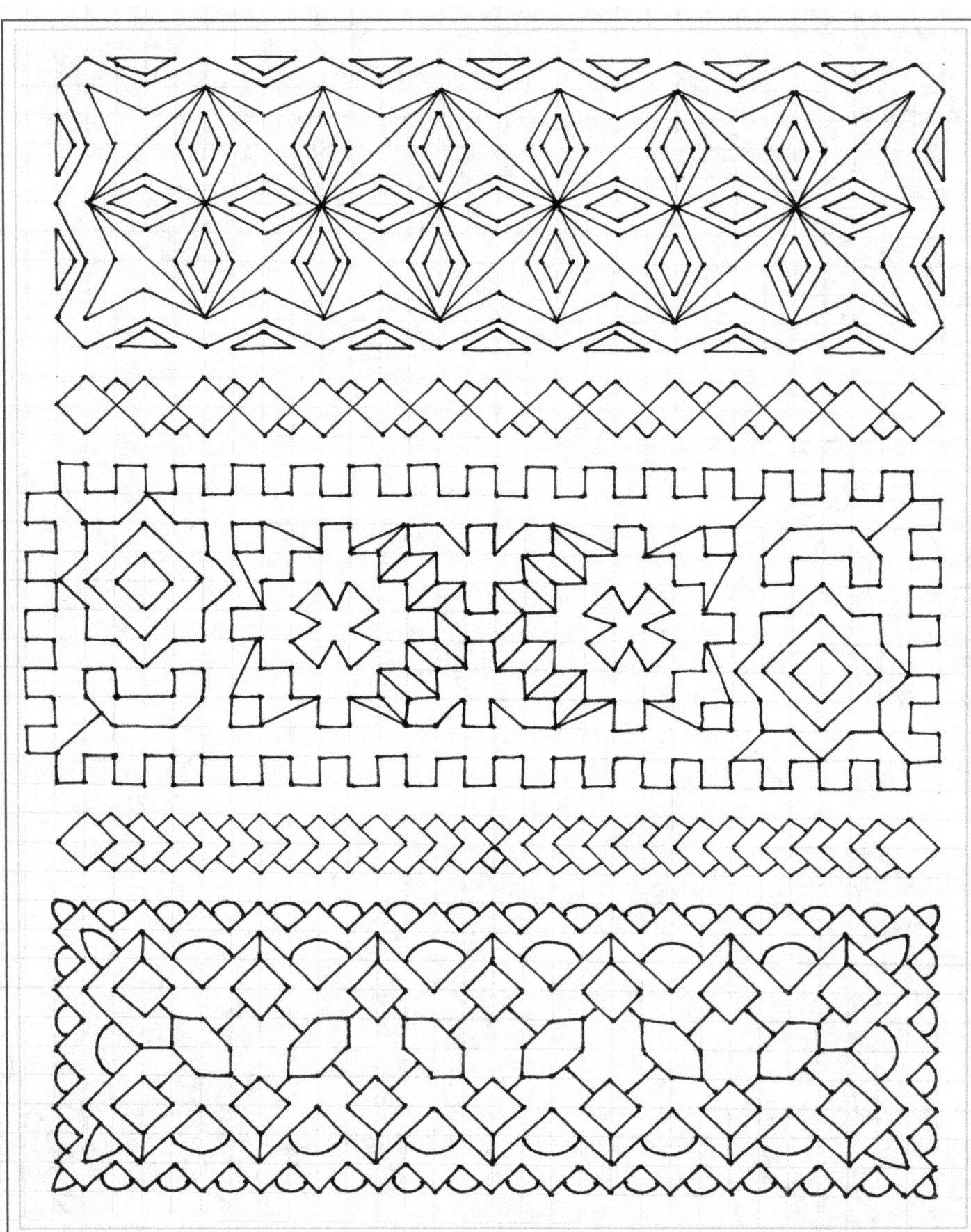

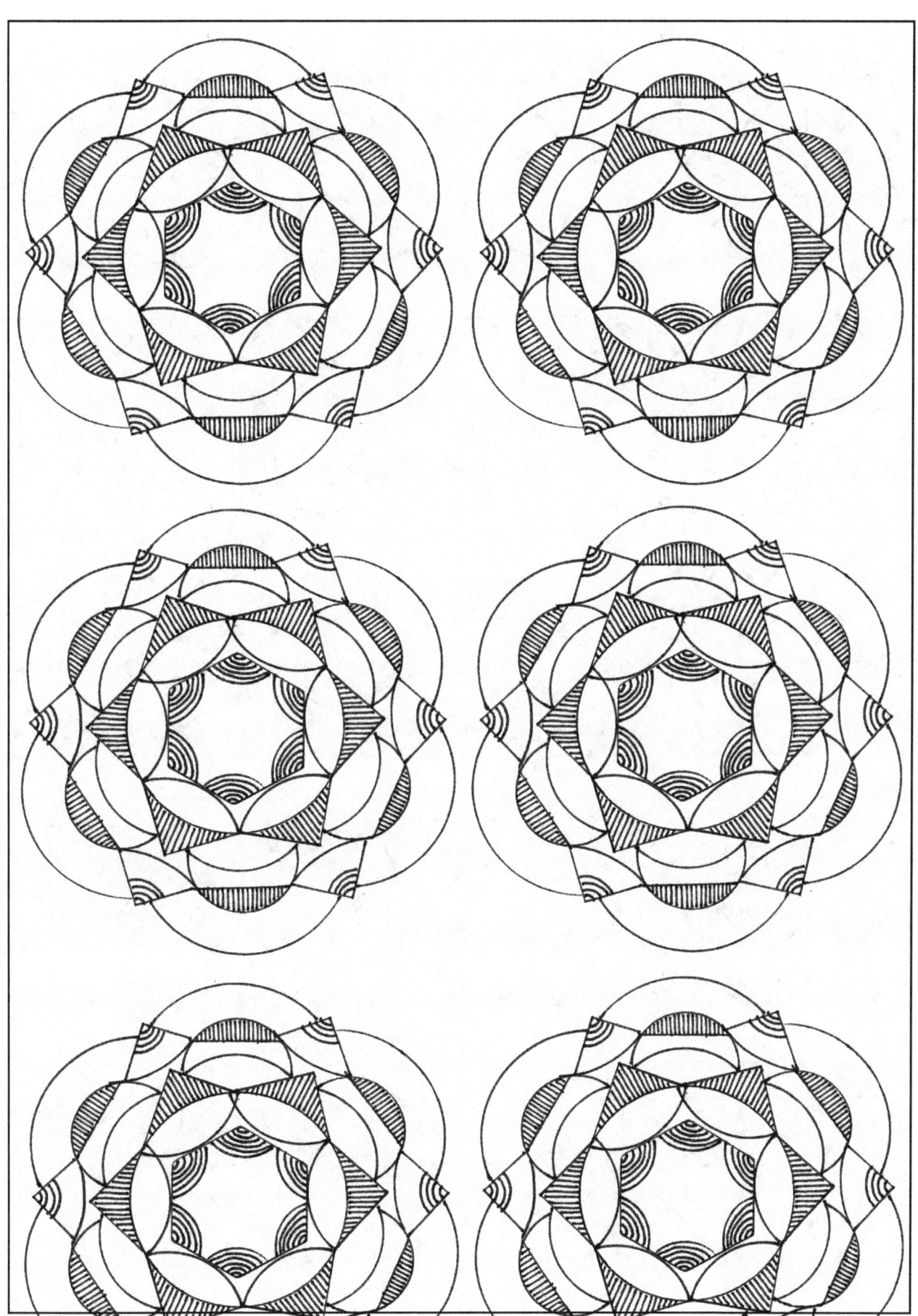

53

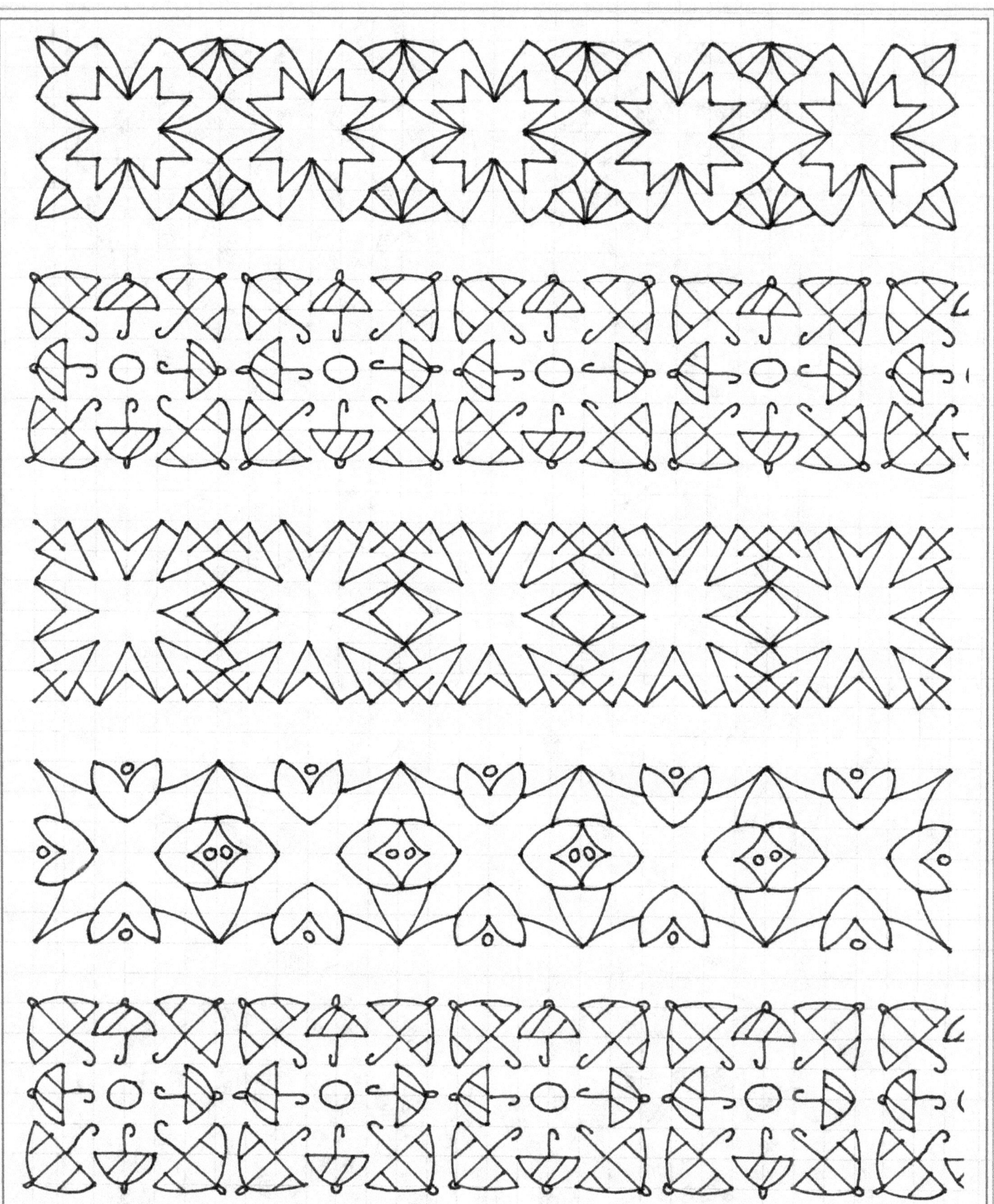

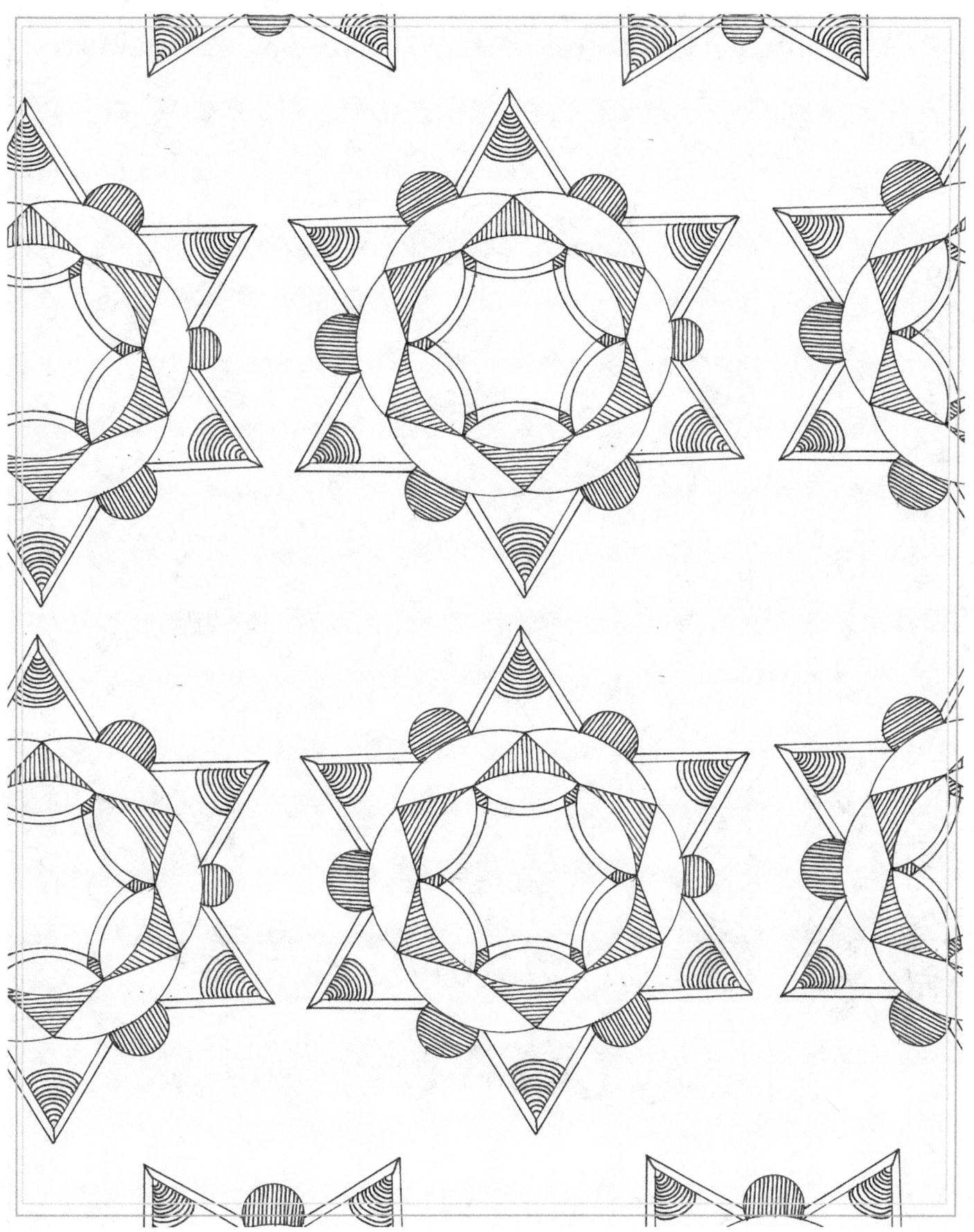

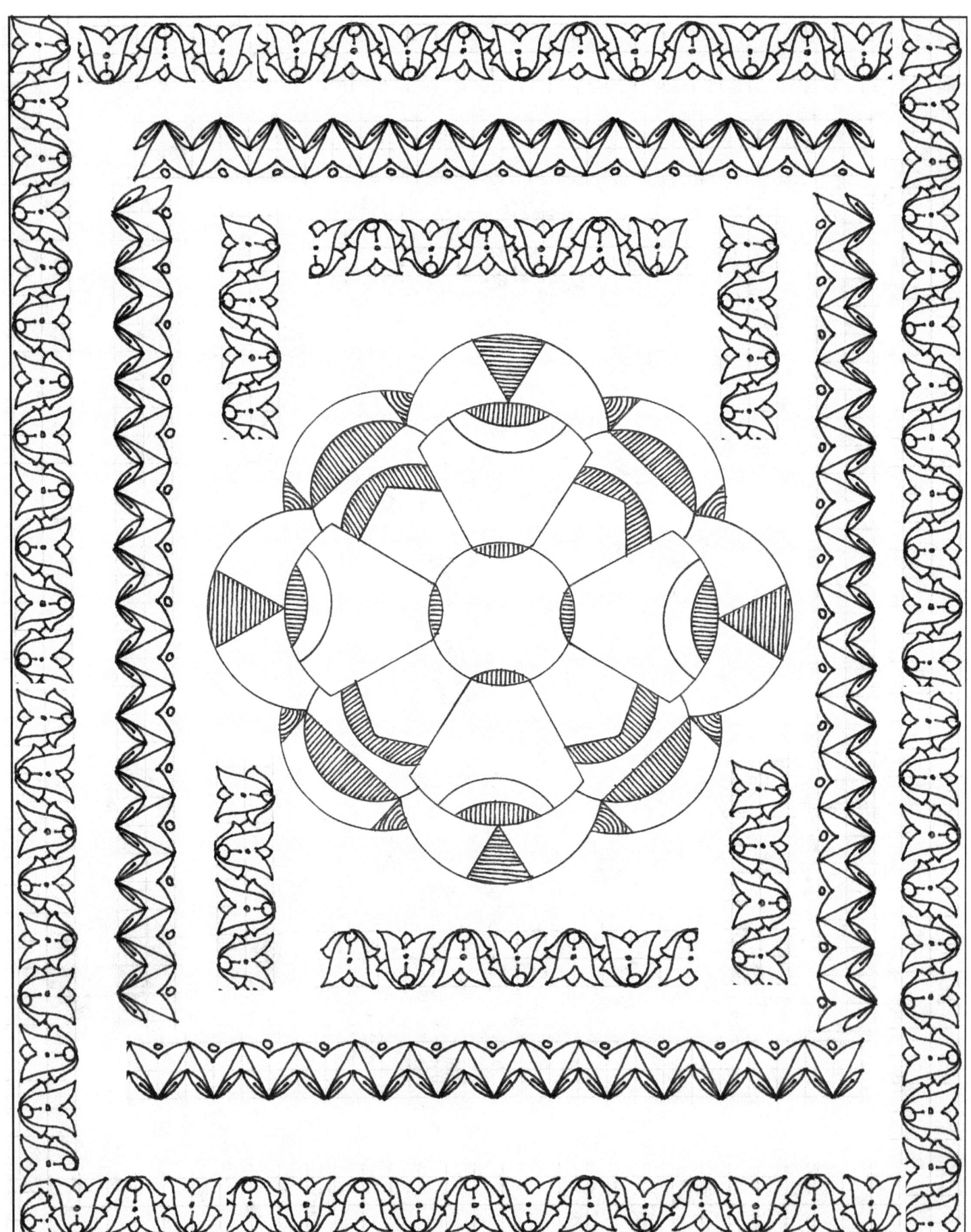

56

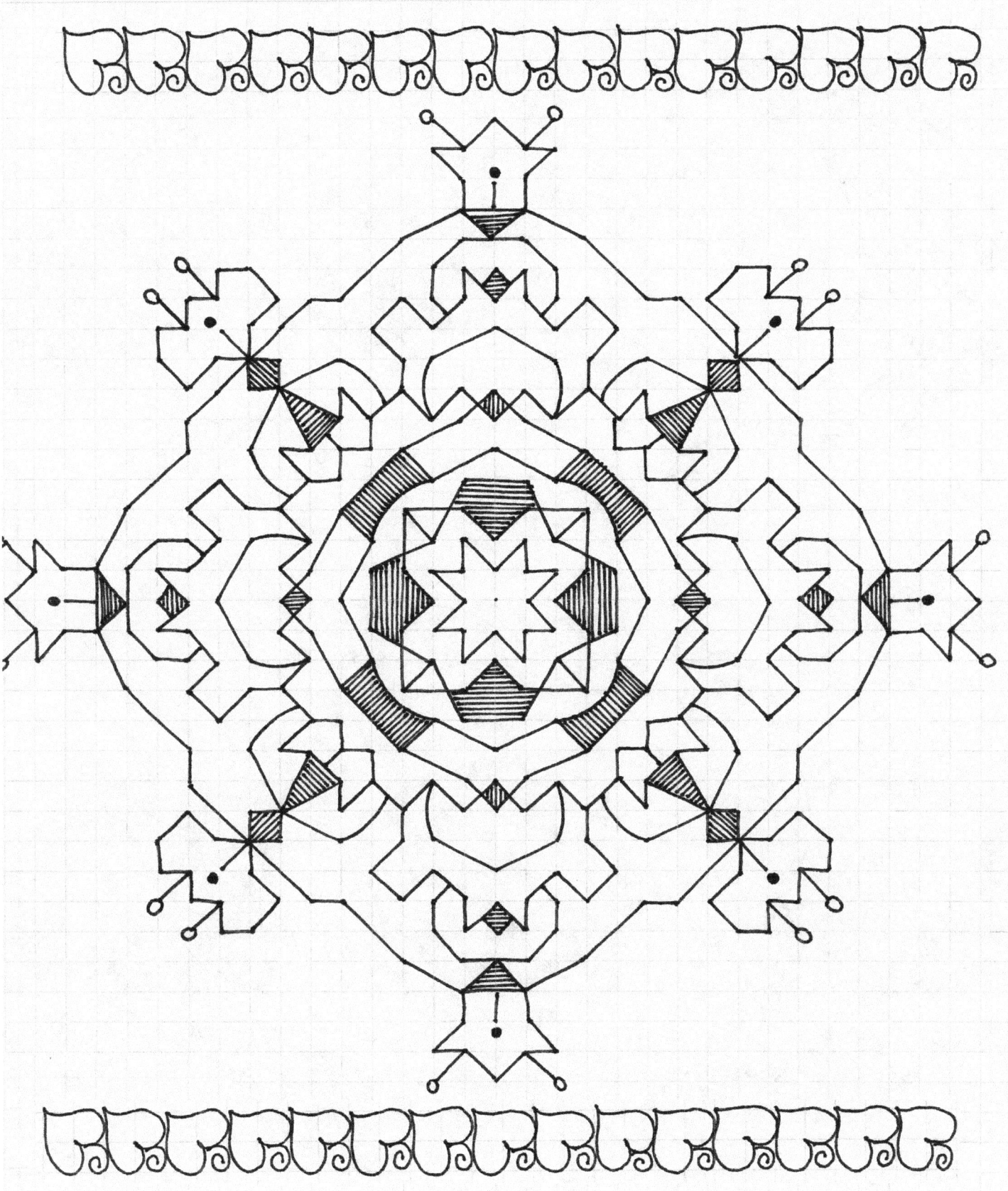

57

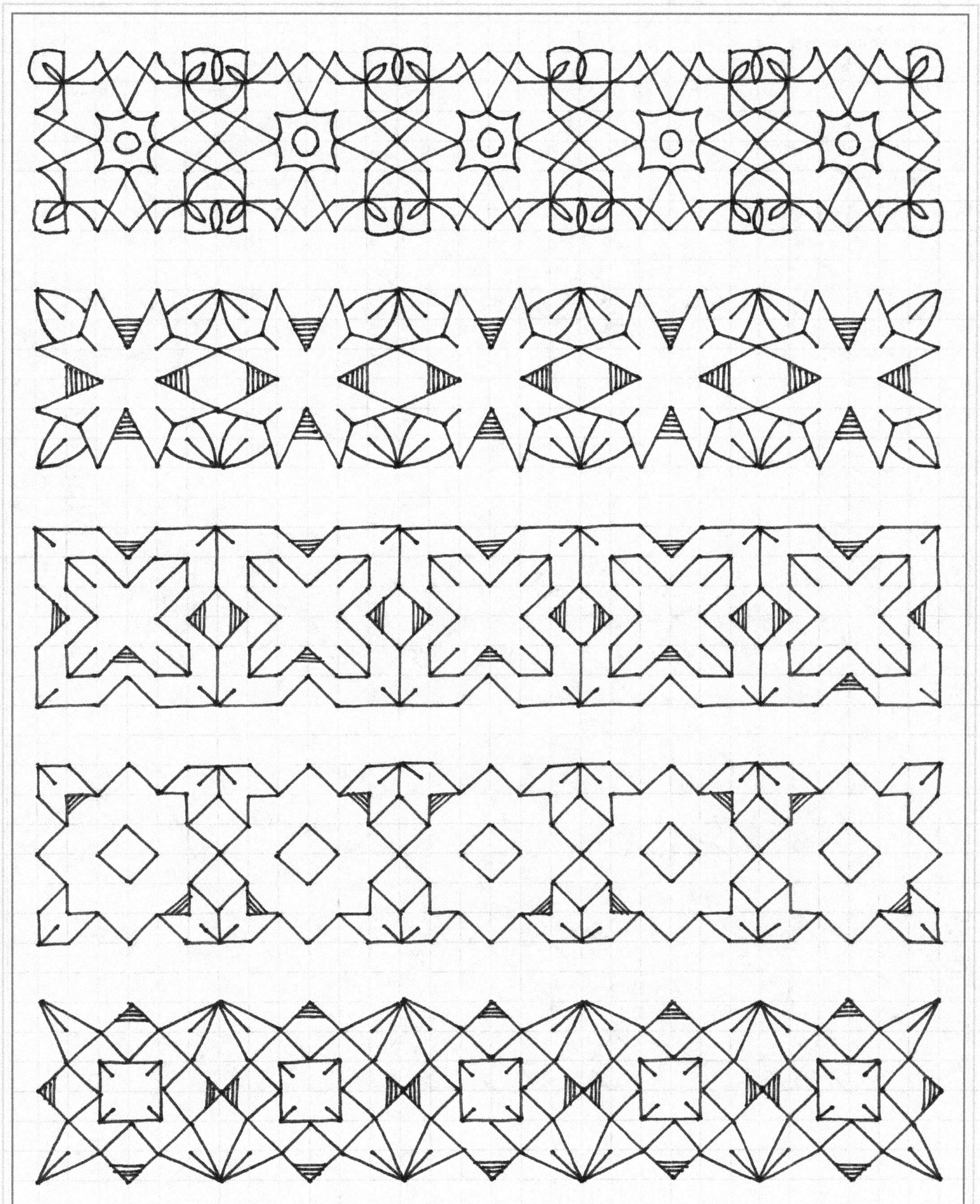

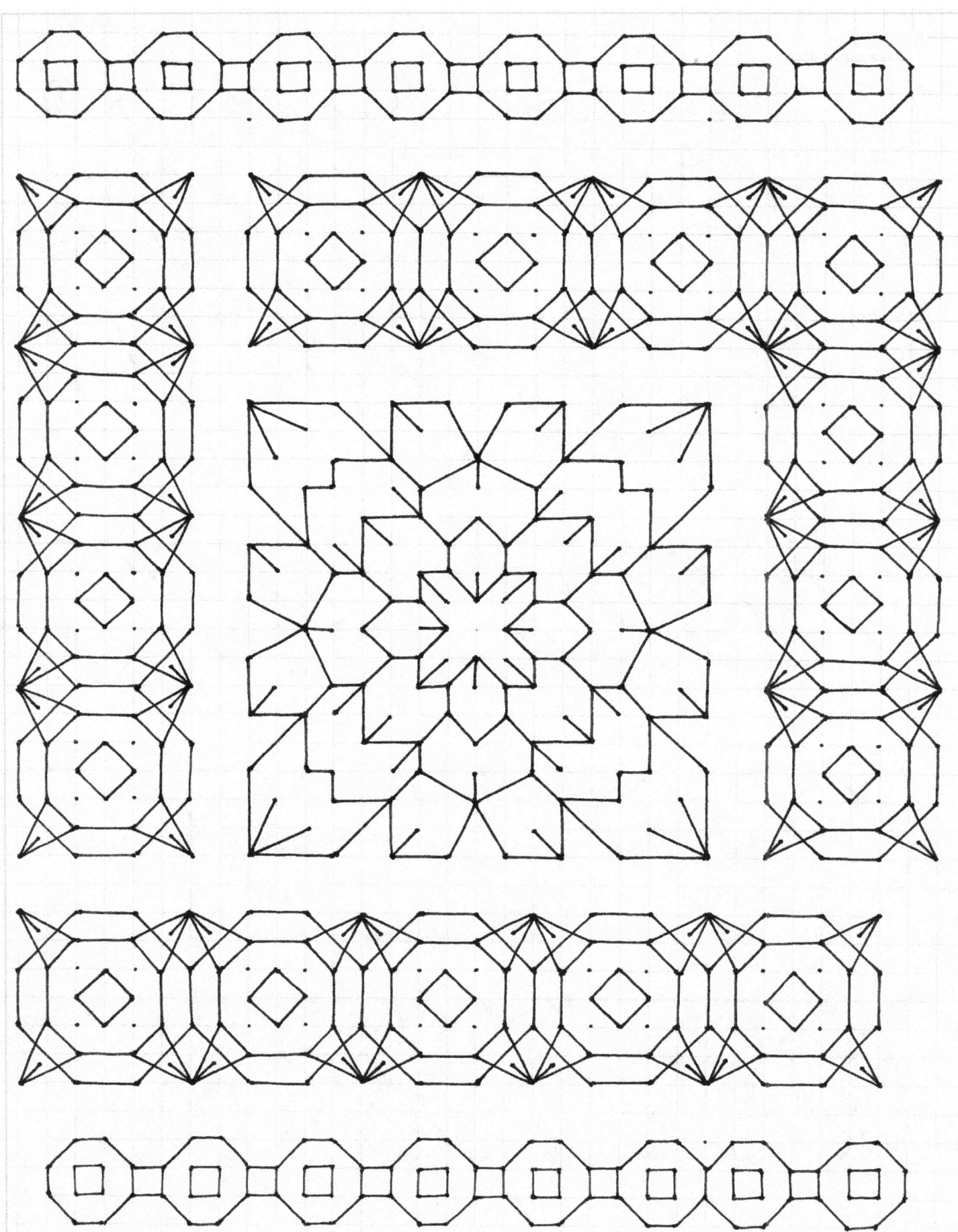

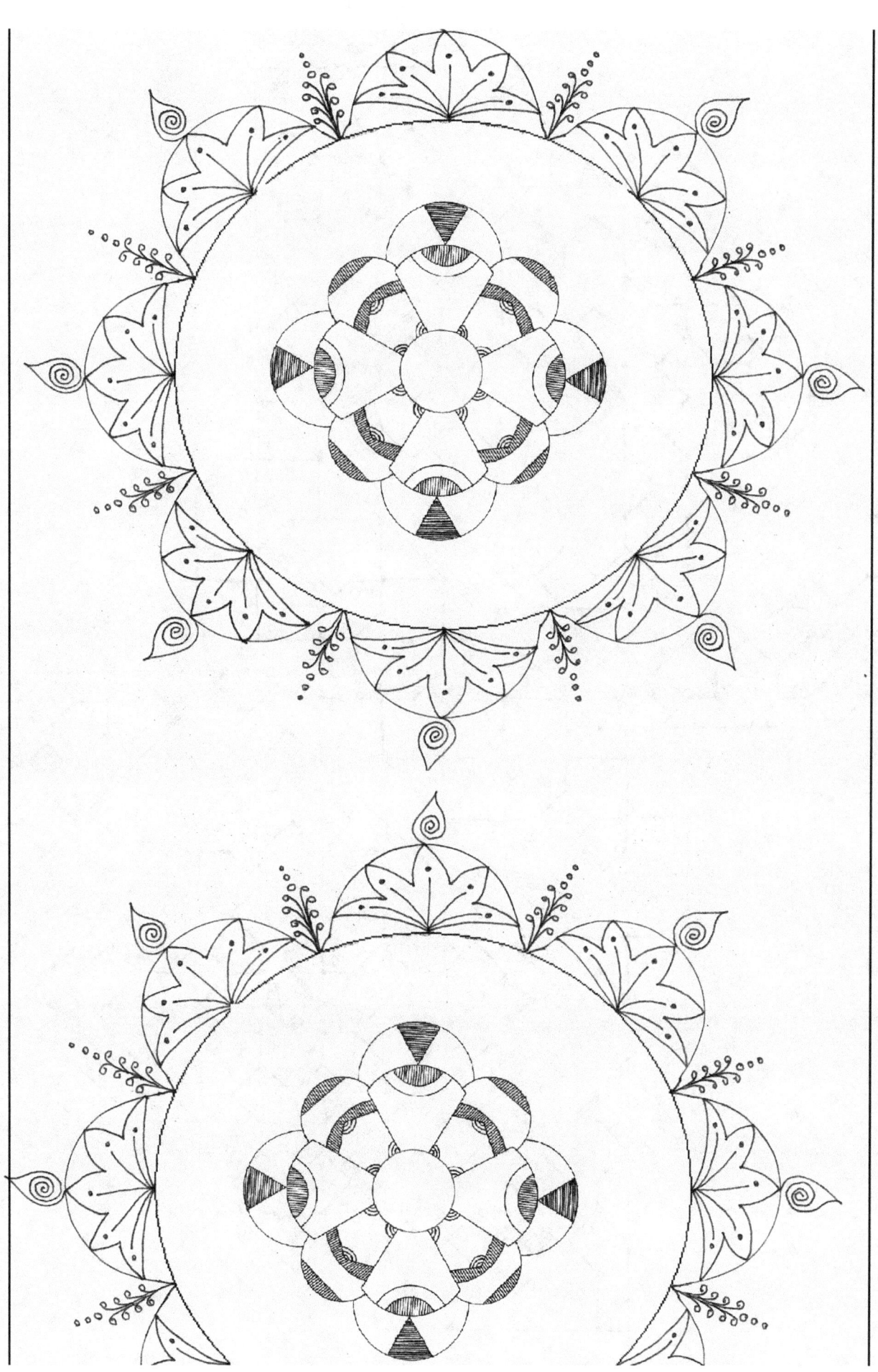

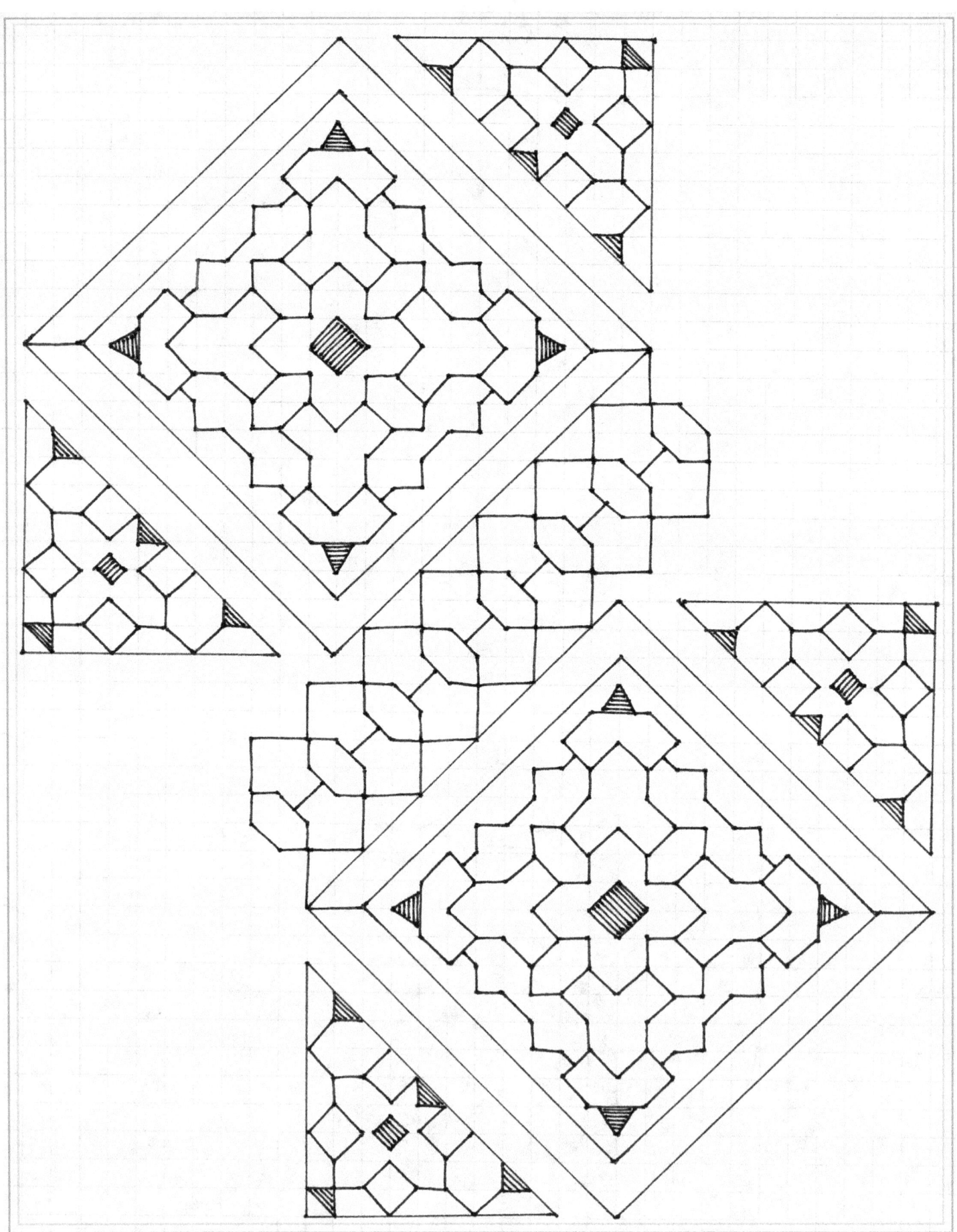

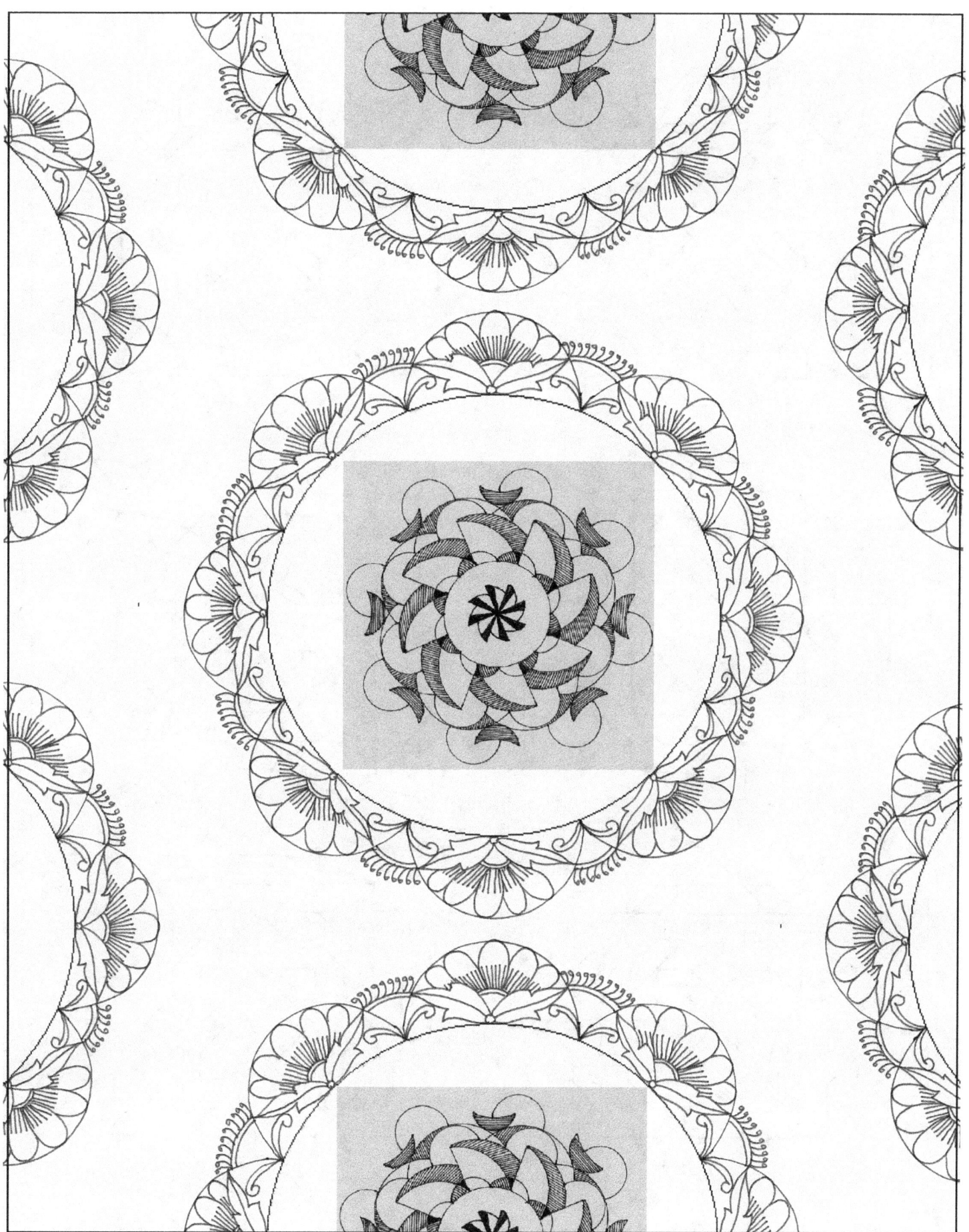

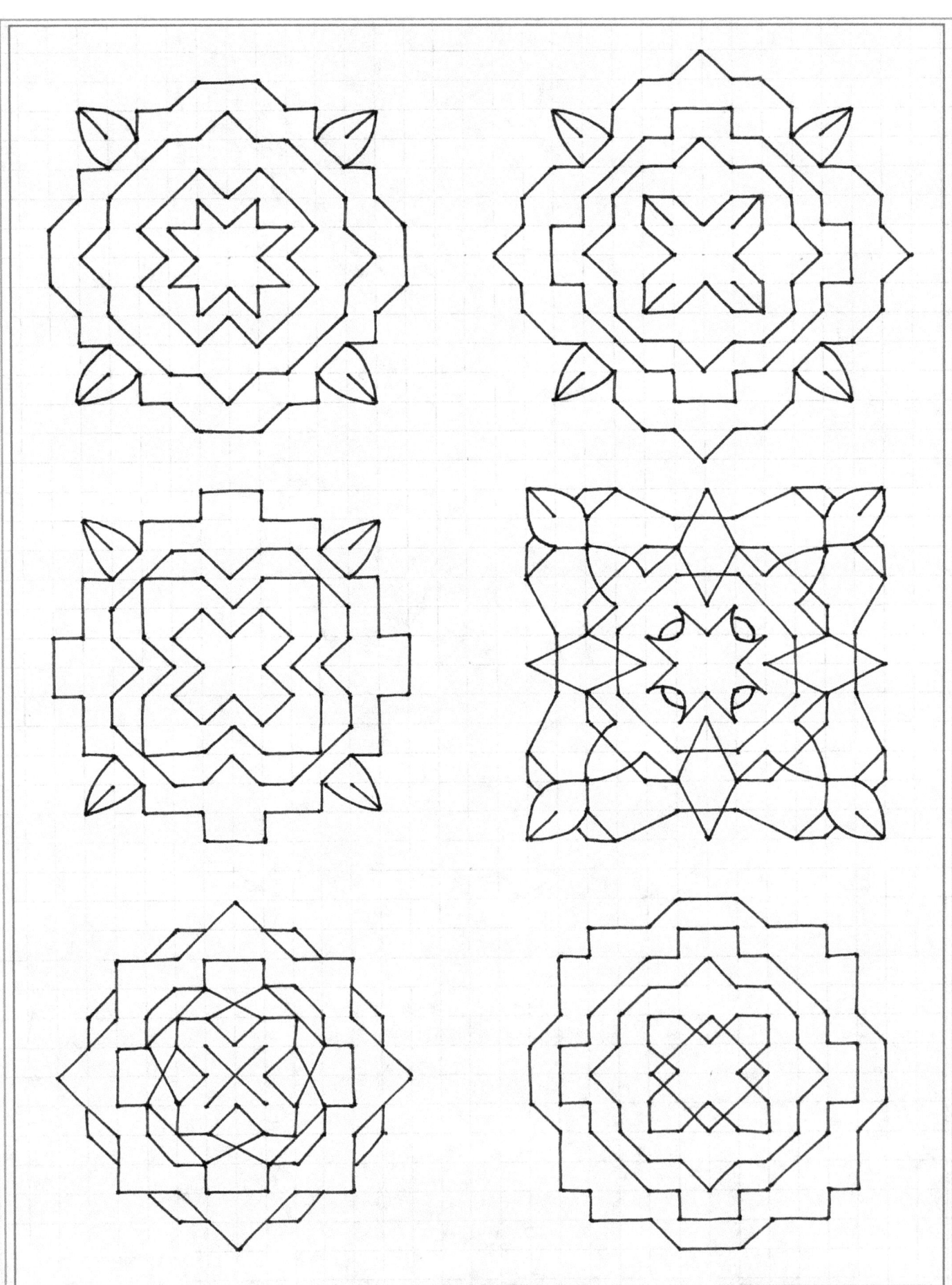

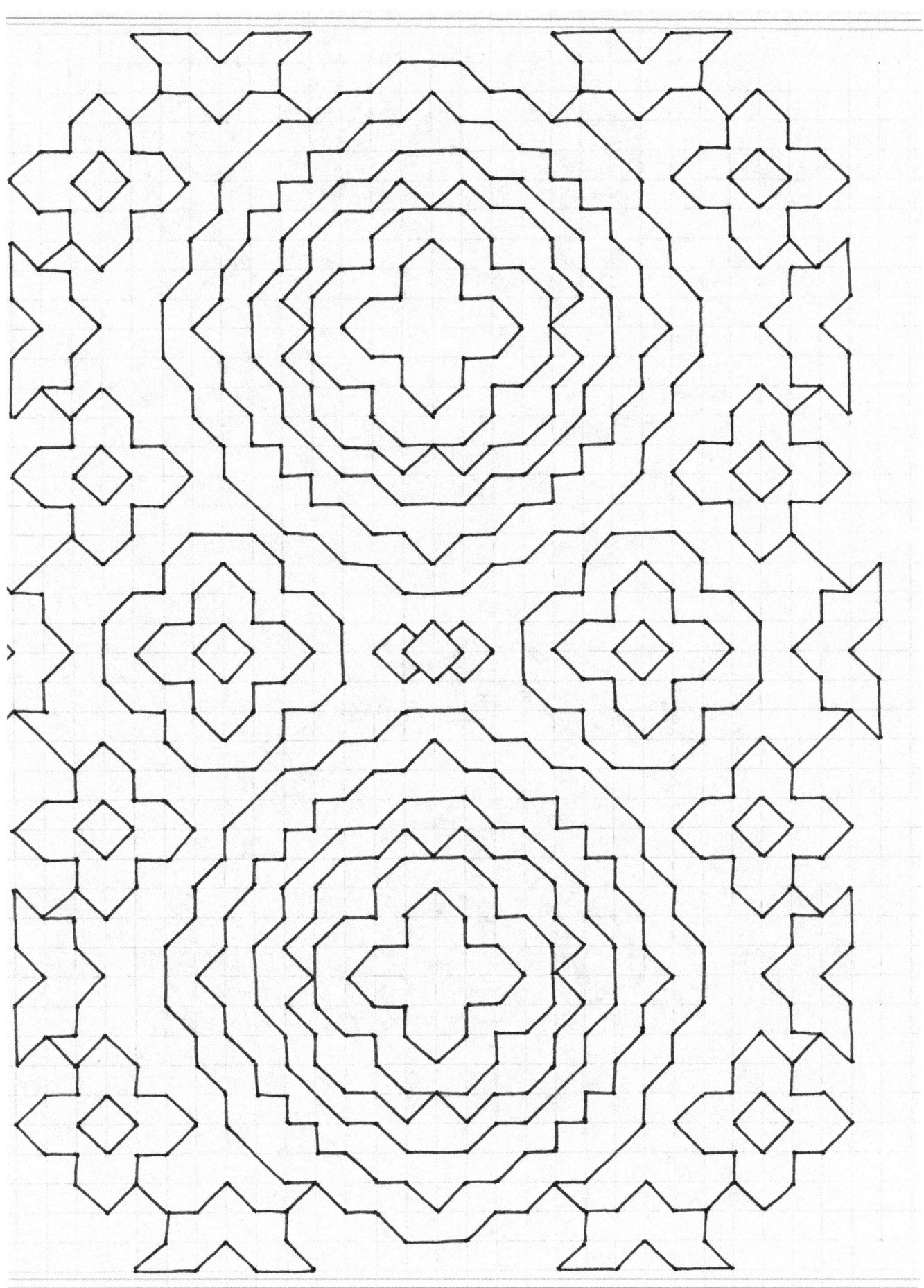

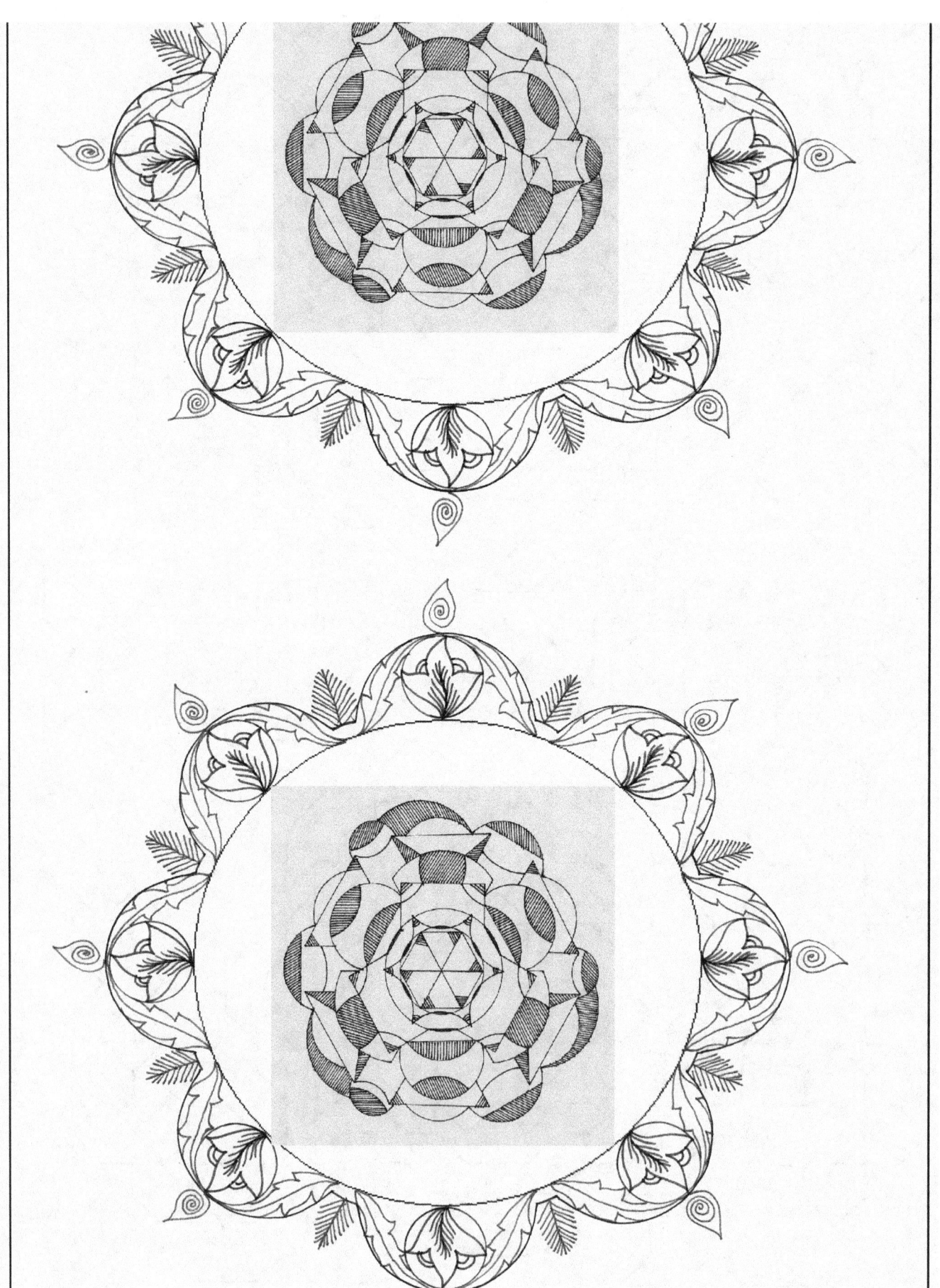

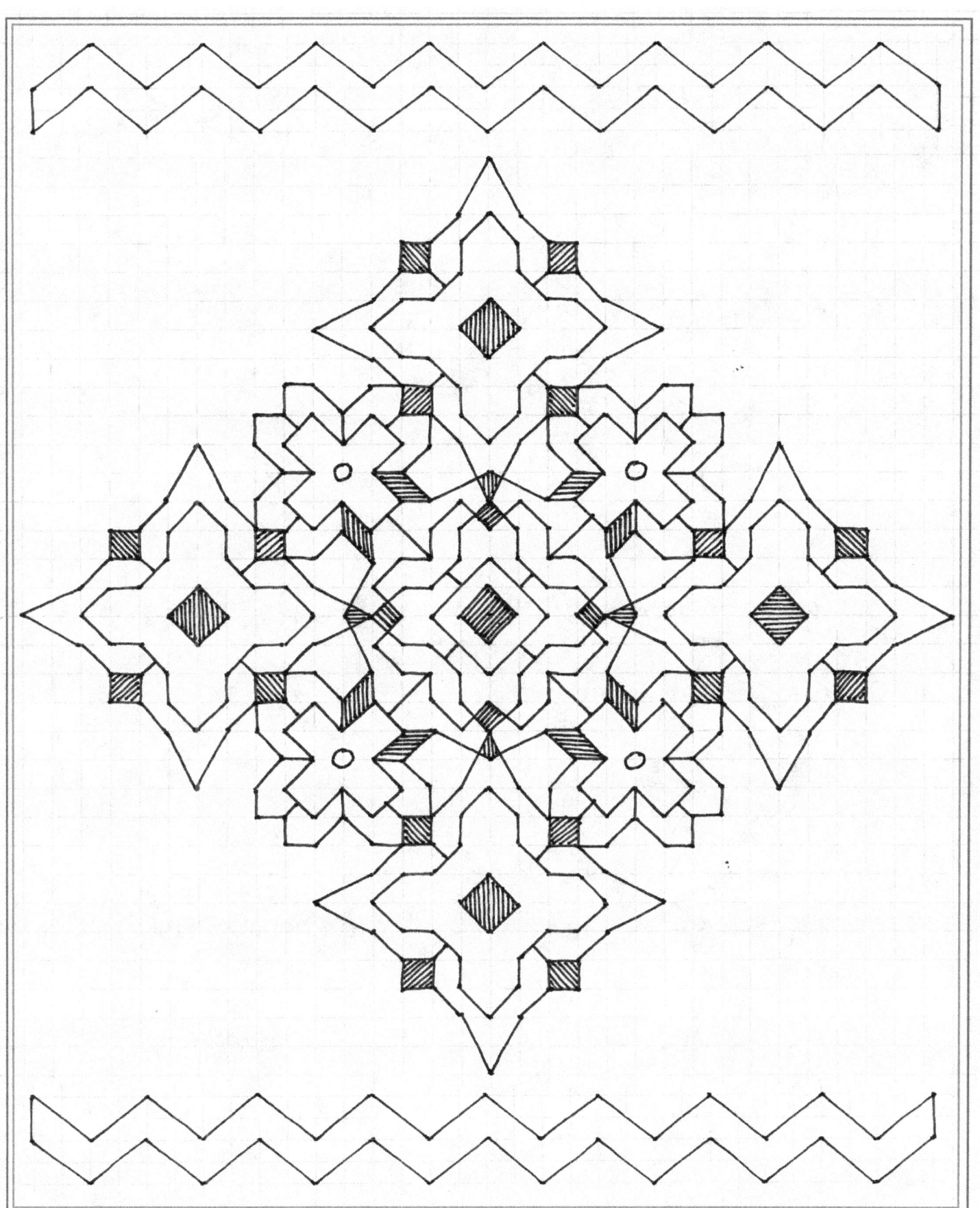

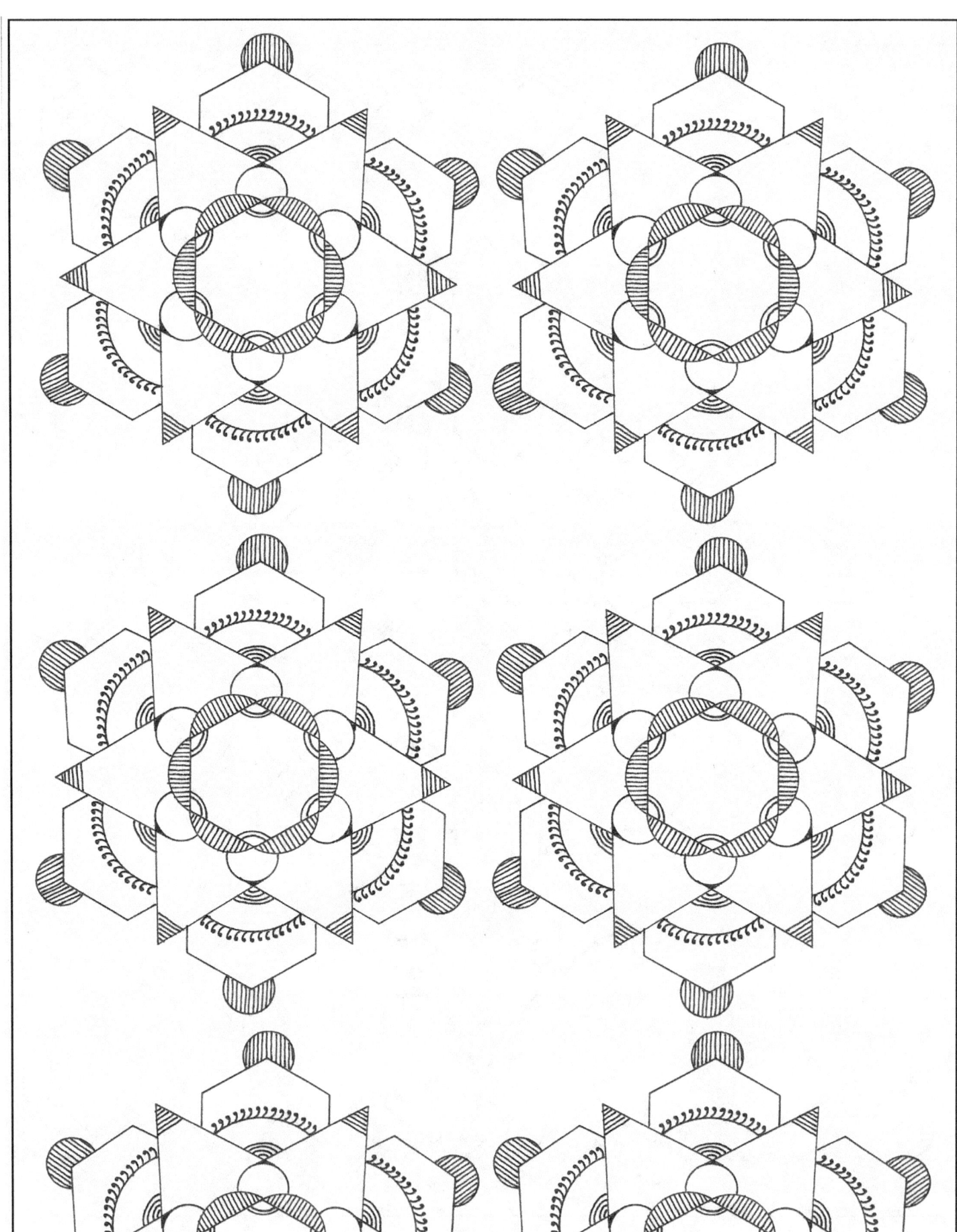

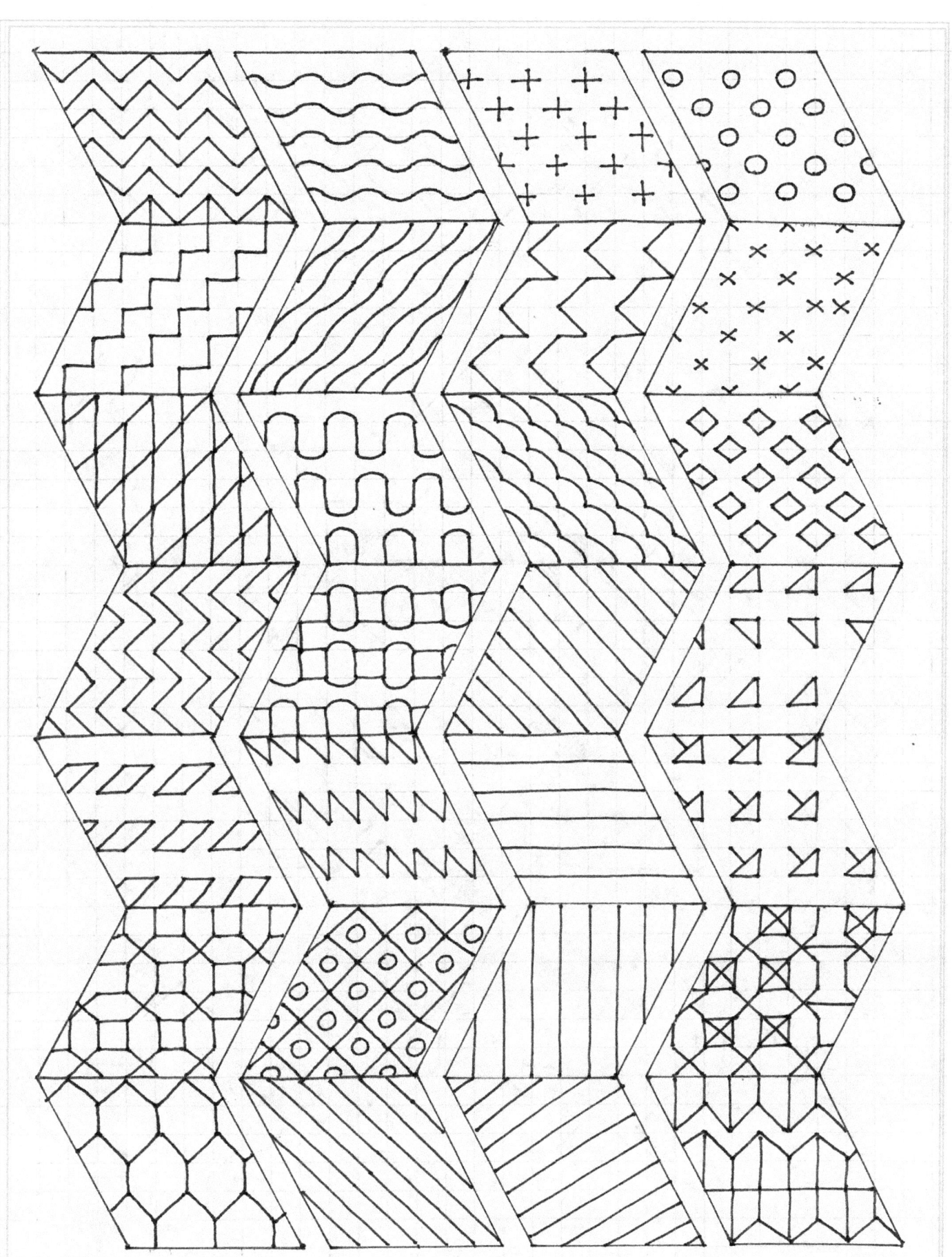

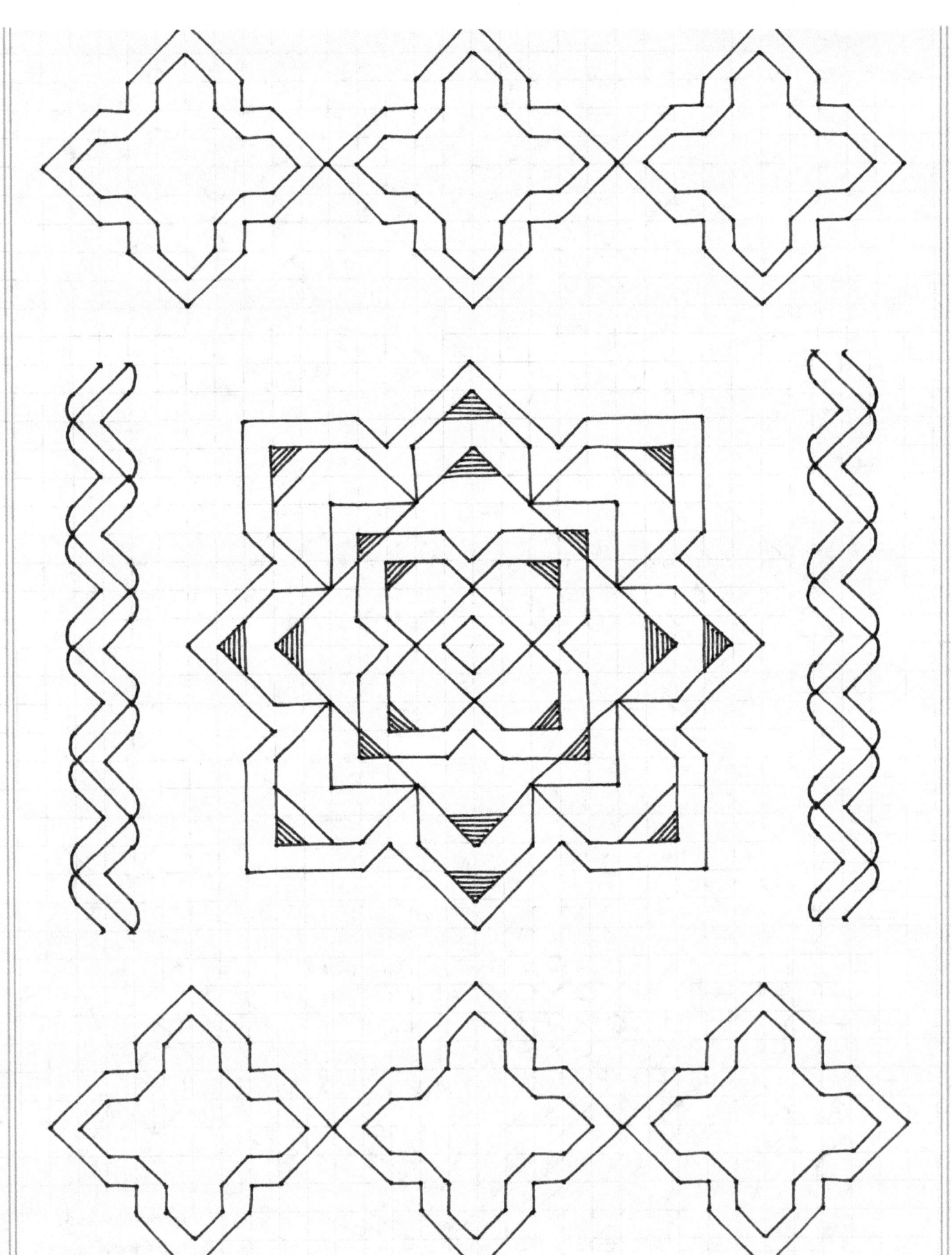

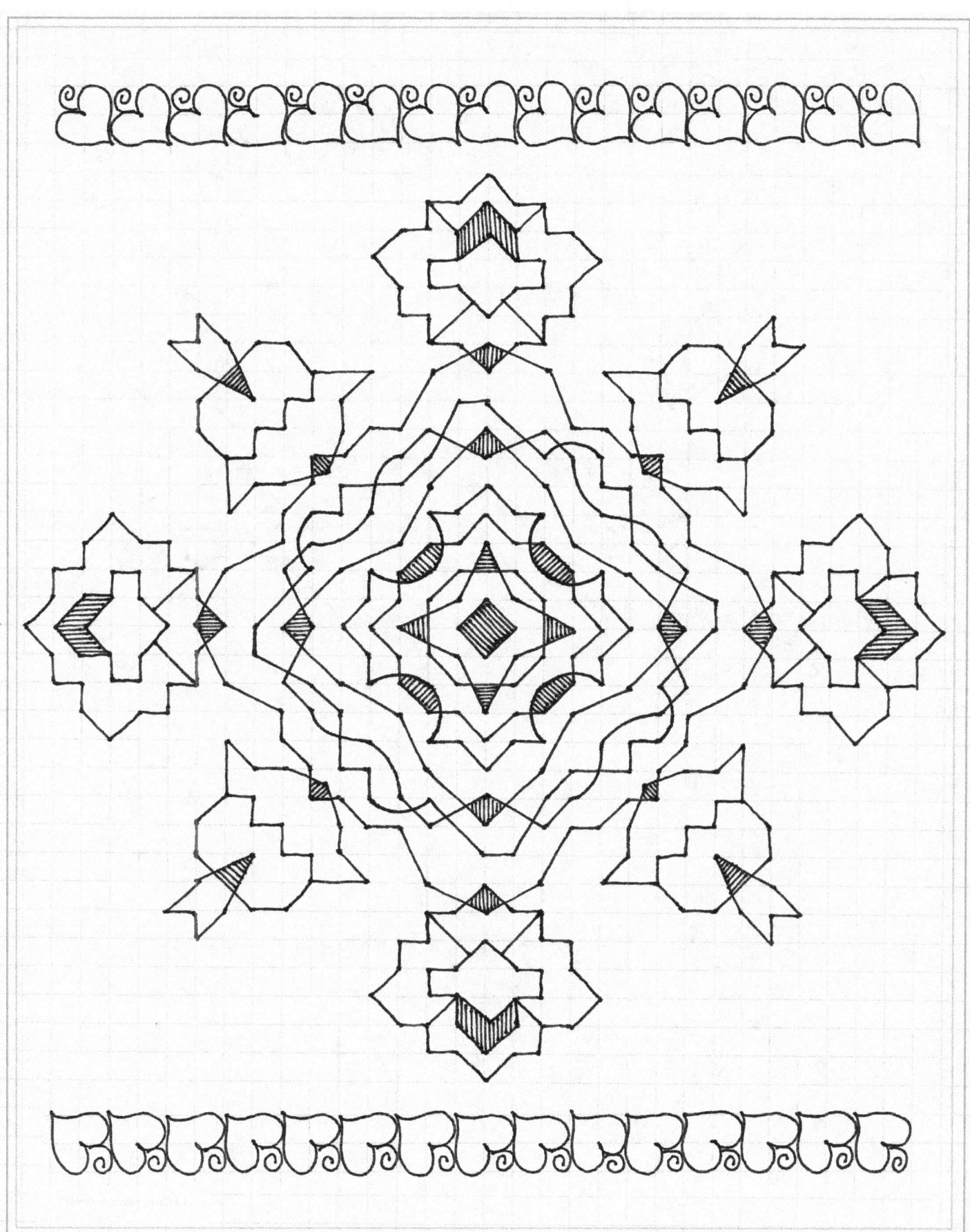

71

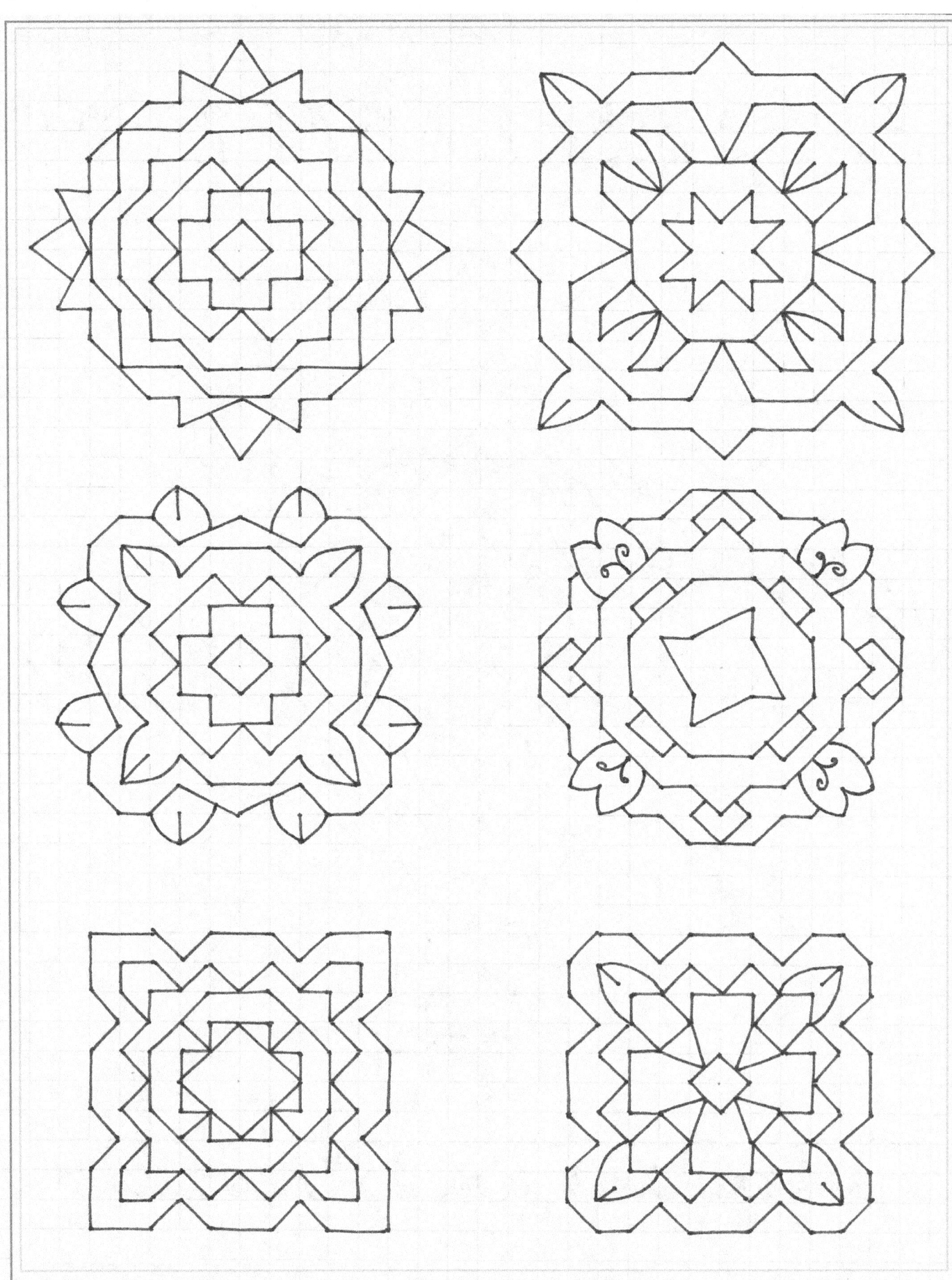

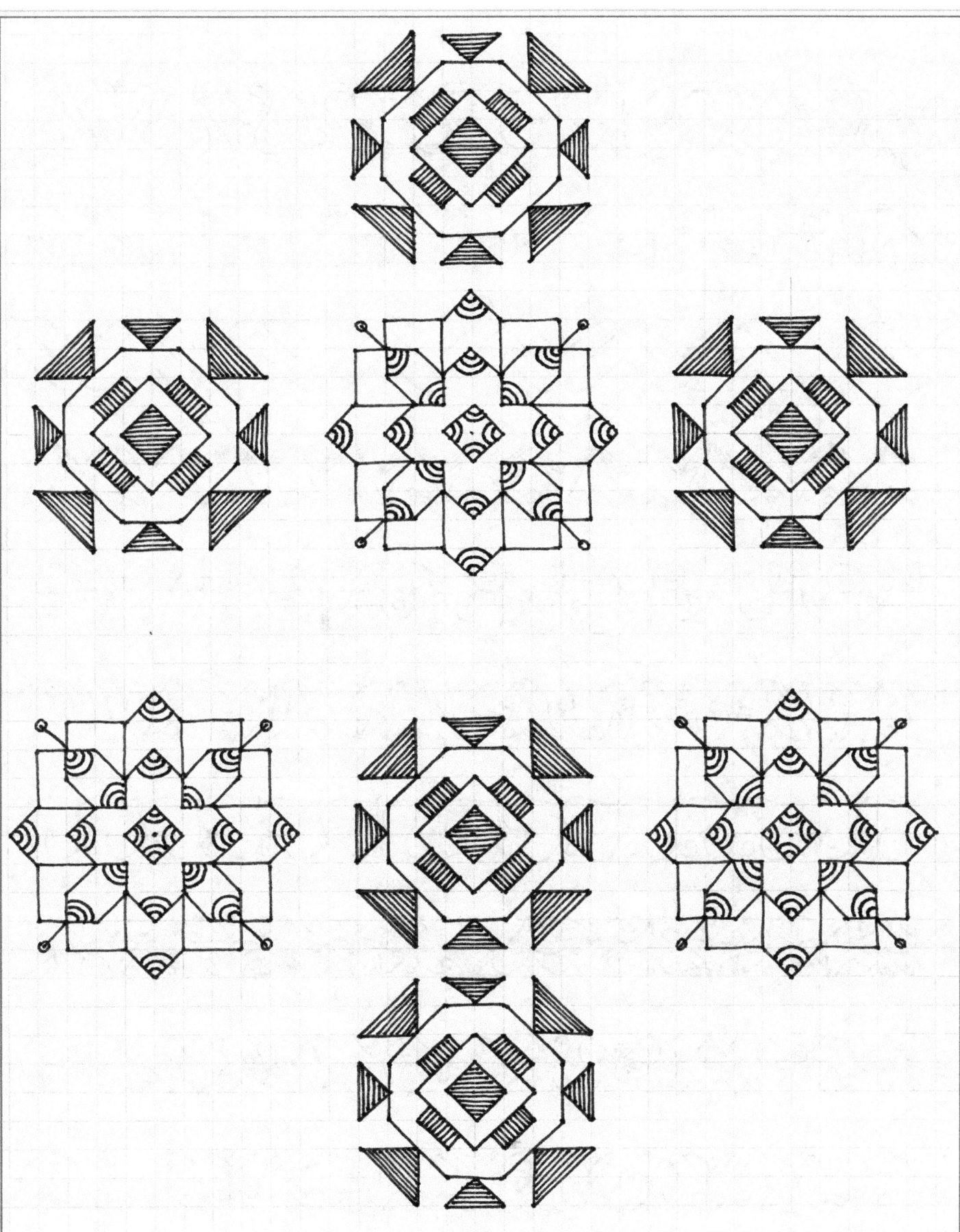

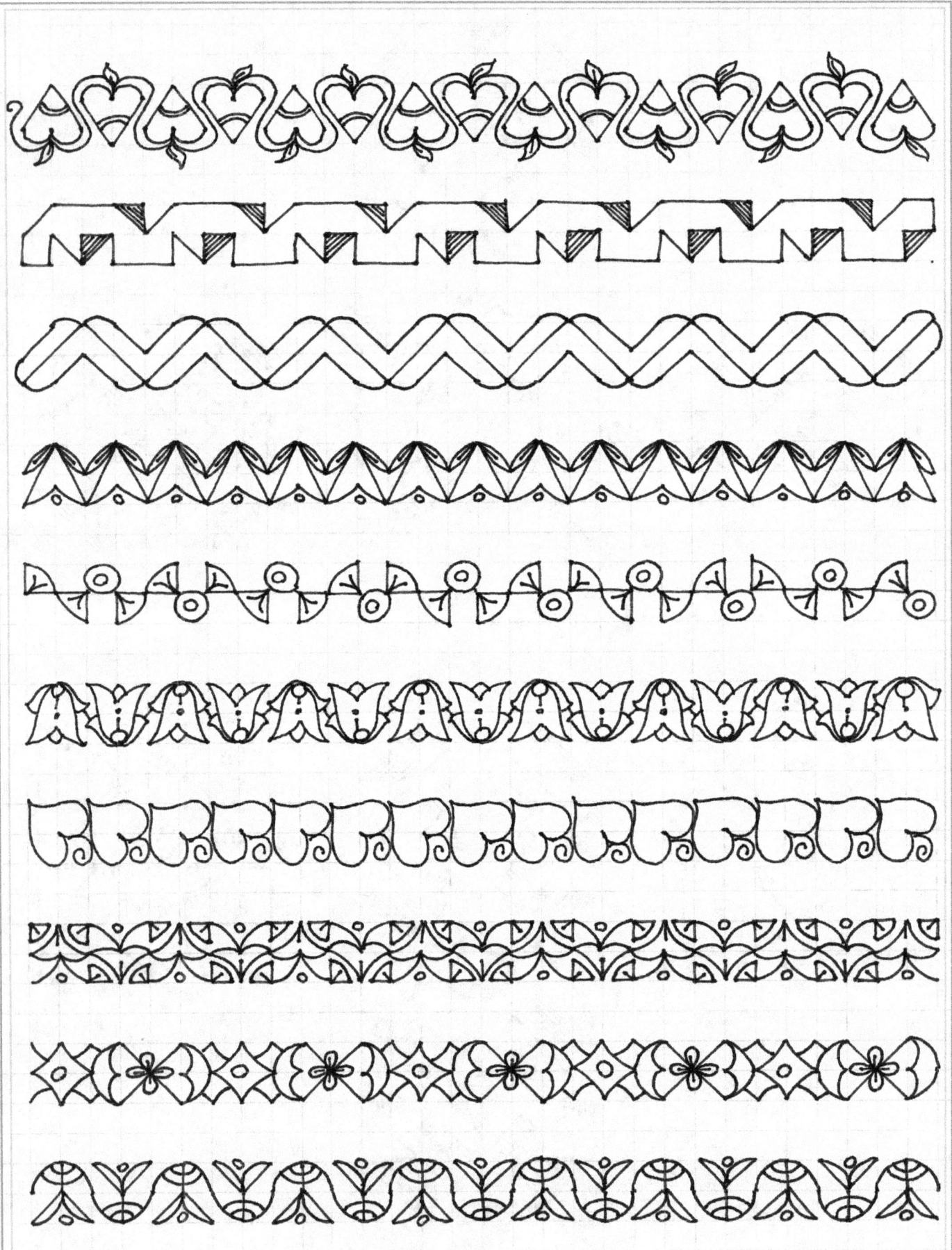

74

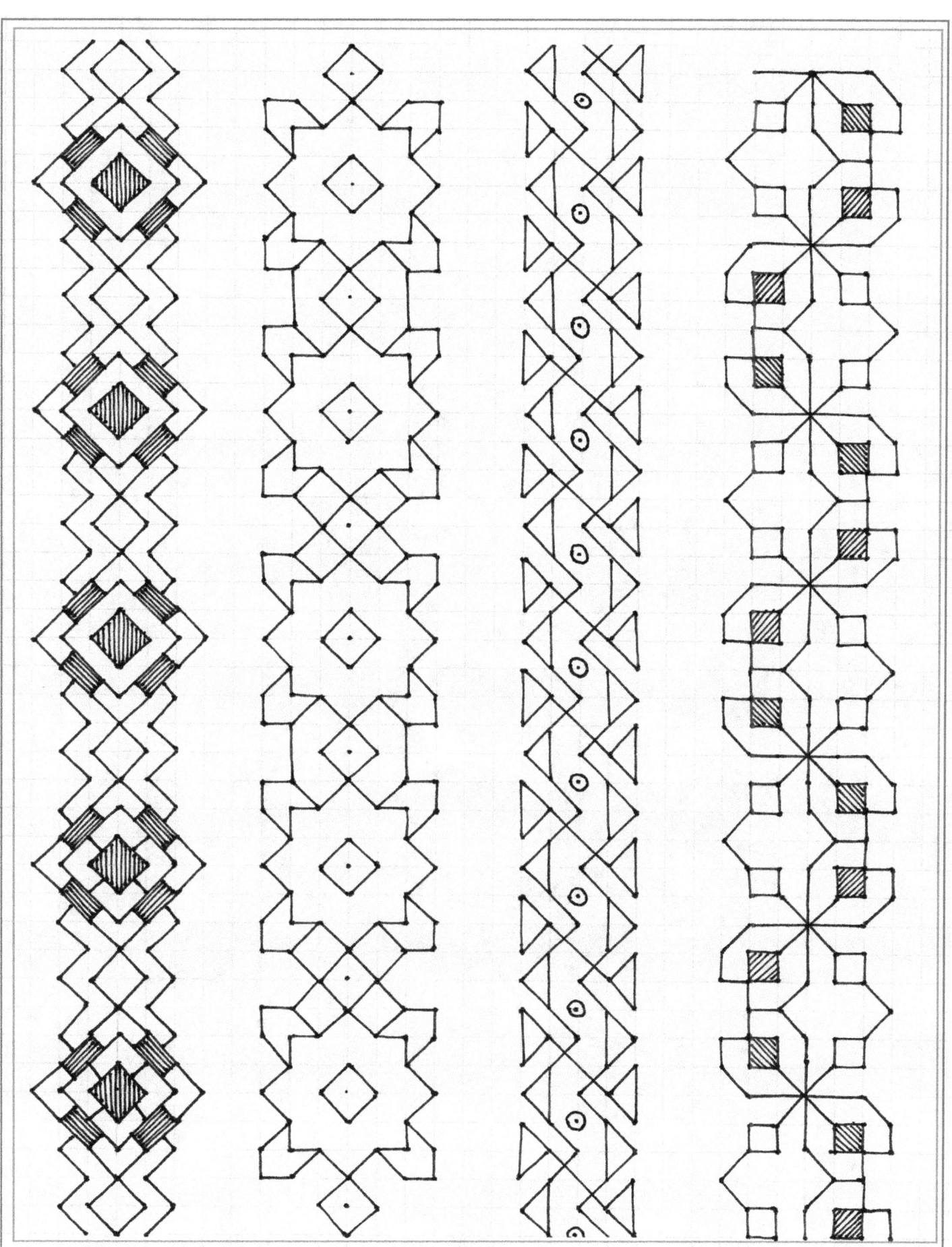

75

About the Author

While I try to stretch my memory, I can't recall the one thing that possibly triggered me to decode the web of my imagination on a piece of paper. My ability to sketch and make designs is one childhood passion that has grown with me. Be it a long train journey or a short bus ride, I always used pen and paper to sketch symmetrical graphics, which are, at times, concrete and sometimes abstract.

Creativity, passion, and perseverance have been constant companions in my journey to depict, represent, and render the throbbing imaginative narratives that I conceptualized in my mind from time to time. In this collection, I bring together several memories of yesteryears and take you along on my voyage during the past decades through my design and sketches. I have never formally attended any school of fine arts, but I do have my share of inspirations.

My mother has been my biggest source of inspiration. Facing the most unpleasant of situations, be as it may, my mother always came up with the most unique, compelling, and out-of-the-box solution to outsmart the situation. This has helped in bringing out the best in me. I constantly aspire to do my best.

My father is a perfectionist. I have grown up observing him repair his cycle, make a kite for all of us siblings, and work with large numbers without calculators! He has always been a constant source of inspiration and motivation for me. Through him, I have learned the art of accomplishing any task, no matter how small or big, with complete devotion and perfection. In creating my designs and sketches, I require both these values, which I have inherited from my father.

Aayush, my school-going son, has been a true friend and a source of inspiration. His love, affection, and trust in me have indeed motivated me. His sincere and honest feedback on my creations has helped me improve and better myself. He does have some sparkling contributions to this project.

This book is dedicated to my parents for putting up a brave front through all odds and for their sheer efforts in overcoming all hardships and for shaping me into a person that I am today.

I hope you enjoy!

Happy coloring!

www.ingramcontent.com/pod-product-compliance
Lightning Source LLC
Chambersburg PA
CBHW081053170526
45165CB00006B/2268